KILL
OR GET
KILLED

The Marketing Killer Instinct

KILL
OR GET
KILLED

The Marketing Killer Instinct

KOLAWOLE OYEYEMI

TP House

KILL OR GET KILLED: **The Marketing Killer Instinct**

Request for information on this title should be addressed to
Kolawole Oyeyemi
Plot 14, Olugbesan Close, off Allen Avenue, Ikeja, Lagos, Nigeria
Email: kolawoo@gmail.com
+234 703 000 1967, +234 803 200 2362.

Library of Congress Cataloging-in-Publication Data

Kolawole Oyeyemi
KILL OR GET KILLED: The Marketing Killer Instinct
ISBN-13: 978-0-9850815-9-1 (Paperback)
ISBN-10: 0-9850815-9-7 (Paperback)
1. Education - Business - Non-fiction 1. Title

Library of Congress Control Number: 2014940072

Edited by Winnie Aduayi
Designed by Trendy Graphics Dept.

Published in Dallas Texas by TP House. A registered trademark of
Trendy Communication llc. www.trendyafrica.com info@trendyafrica.com

Printed in the United States of America

DEDICATION

There is a benefit in practically every experience humanity is either compelled to go through or elects to go through. This book is the product of the benefit of an experience I had been privileged to go through. It is therefore dedicated first to God for His uncommon grace and mercy upon my life. I am one of the most blessed men on earth! Thank you Lord for everything. I will be eternally grateful.

The next dedication goes to the persons who occasioned the experience. In 2012, somebody threw me a challenge during a conversation around my fourth book: Wealth Without Theft. He challenged me to write a book on Marketing. At the point of that conversation, I didn't give it much thought.

However, on 3rd March 2013, another conversation held between a colleague and I, who reminded me of the earlier conversation where someone had asked that I write a book on Marketing. He expressed his view that there was a need for such a book based on certain experiences by some folks he knew.

That conversation was the turning point. I drove home from that meeting thinking about the conversation, and it dawned on me that I may have some materials and competence to write something people may find useful, either as practicing marketers or non-marketing people who need to have some understanding of how to work around marketing issues that they may be dealing with in their enterprises. This book is the end product of both conversations.

AKNOWLEDGEMENT

This book is the product of over twenty three years of practice across industries, long hours of classroom study in various professional and business schools across the world, personal studies, and my leverage on the wealth of many excellent marketing war generals I have been privileged to work with. I am most grateful to all who have added to my marketing knowledge and competences.

In addition to those who impacted my knowledge and practice significantly enough to be indirectly responsible for this work, I must also acknowledge several people who agreed to be interviewed and encouraged this work with their invaluable contributions from Lagos to Johannesburg and Nairobi to Accra. I cannot thank you enough!

I must specially appreciate Sarah Wangiku for opening up her network of friends and family to me, and for being my chaperon, my driver, tour guide, and so much more. You are amazing! Thanks for setting up all those meetings. My stay in Nairobi couldn't have been as eventful without you. Thank you very much for supporting me to give this body of knowledge back to the marketing and business community.

My special thanks goes to my wife Adenike, and my children, Boluwatife, Oluwademilade and Temiloluwa for being my friends, critics and support. I couldn't have done this without you guys.

To all my mentors, colleagues, seniors, staff, contemporaries and any other person I have been privileged to learn from, including those I have had to practice my little knowledge on, thanks for allowing me to learn from you, and to sometimes get on your nerves.

Thank you all.

Kolawole Oyeyemi

"

The approach that will win the hearts and minds of customers leverages content and context to create marketing that intersects with a customer's lifestyle, needs and interests.

"

– Brian halligan, CEO Hubspot.

CAVEAT

Accessing marketing data is a tough business in most parts of Africa. There is no central repository of verified or validated knowledge for ease of accessibility. There is also no recognized and industry-wide acceptable body to validate data about brands, categories and markets. Scholars or researchers are therefore, constrained to depend on individuals or practitioners who are willing to speak, and some documented evidences that cannot be validated by unbiased industry umpires.

The cases discussed in this book should be seen from this perspective. They are outputs of interviews, studies of available and accessible data, and my interpretations of same. This explains why I have refrained from quoting hard data, but extracted the marketing strategy lessons from the brands' stories. Errors of omission or commission are not intended, and therefore regretted, as there are no institutional validators.

FOREWORD

The World Economic Forum on Africa held in Abuja, Nigeria, from 7-9 May 2014. So it is Africa's turn. The much touted 'Africa Rising' will manifest most potently in the consumer marketplace, where determined foreign investors who have been waiting on the wings all of these years take on entrenched multinationals, many of whom will adopt an unyielding stance. Not to mention the mushrooming of homegrown African brands with an indomitable 'I no go gree' *(won't give in)* spirit. This makes for relevance and perfect timing for 'Kill or Get Killed: The Marketing Killer Instinct' – a case based Afro-centric marketing book that reads like a marketing novel.

However, Kill or Get Killed: The Marketing Killer Instinct, is serious. Some will find this serious novel useful for developing their verbal abilities, others for improving their focus and concentration. Still, others will value it for its entertainment value; but all, in particular, students of and academics in marketing and management, professional marketers, and business leaders, will agree it is as yet the best work on marketing in Africa in general, and Nigeria in particular, offering an outstanding wealth of learning and experience. It is sure to expand one's understanding of what is possible, because it is based on real life brand marketing; case studies of what happened, how and why. The writer was untiring in researching 'the what', scholarly in investigating 'the how' and courageous, some will say, audacious in making deductions on 'the why', whilst daring to make some prescriptions, yes....prescriptions in marketing, along the way.

The range of themes and contexts in the Kill or Get Killed: The Marketing Killer Instinct, and the learning and teaching opportunities they present are breathtaking. The controversies they must generate are even more exciting. Starting with the 'Can any good thing come out of Lagos Traffic?' The writer narrates how he managed to write this 'Kill or Get Killed' book, as he watched brands wrestle each other to the ground in the Lagos traffic. Something good came out of the Lagos traffic and something else, even better, came out – an appreciation of the importance of the street hawker as a route-to-market in many categories, at least in Nigeria. After whetting the appetite with a few global lessons – the MCI vs AT&T struggle for market share; the mix of logic and magic in marketing discipline and practice; the challenge of nailing a moving target in marketing; admitting to our being able to often see no more than the tip of the iceberg of consumer needs; the danger of using market research data the way a drunkard uses a lamp-post at night *(to lean on rather than to see the way home)*; not waiting till it is broken before fixing marketing problems; the challenge of differentiation in an industry like Telecommunications faced with commoditization pressures – the writer offers a few African marketing homilies, notably the probable role of liveries and their consistency in winning (and losing) brand wars in Africa; about Africans and their emotional connections.

The writer left the richest stuff for the middle to the end. The fascinating Milk War between Promasidor Cowbell and WAM-CO Peak Milk, still ongoing, is so well rendered it is perfect case paper for teaching and learning about challenger strategies of an outflanking nature, using all four elements of the marketing mix. The Cowbell blitzkrieg on the Mallam's table for a dominant share of stocking, display and POS deployment, like never before and not since, also demonstrates how to integrate marketing, sales and channel development strategies. This is unlike the War of the Stouts and Nigeria Telco War, which show how to set, develop and execute big audacious and hairy goals. There are lots of other case studies from the telecom, stout and lager beers, mobile handset, advertising agency, food and seasonings categories and industries showing how to kill and come back from the dead when brands are at war.

This is Kolawole Oyeyemi, at his best. Drawing from over 22 years of marketing and management experience in leading multinationals across industries, this well celebrated industry icon standing tall on ethics and professional reputation has delivered a killer punch. None of us will ever again be able to lazily complain about the lack of quality literature on marketing in action in Nigeria and out of Nigeria for Africa.

George E Thorpe
Managing Consultant, Market-Space
Director at phd Nigeria
Chairman at HeadstartIT Services Nigeria
Chairman at Roddenberry Nigeria

CONTENTS

AUTHOR'S NOTE

CAN ANY GOOD THING COME OUT OF LAGOS TRAFFIC?

Traffic jams bedevil most mega cities or commercial capitals; New York, Hong Kong and London are examples. Even at the best of times and in situations where good road networks abound, certain periods are known for their peaks in traffic congestion. Lagos, the commercial capital of Nigeria is no exception to this malaise. Most often, sad tales are usually associated with traffic congestions: missed appointments, missed flights, delayed arrivals at important engagements, and sometimes crime. Rarely do you have positive stories told of traffic congestion experiences, except from a marketing point of view.

Traffic congestions in Lagos provide a veritable platform for commerce. I call it Lagos Street Economics. Migrant sales boys and girls with different wares ranging from consumables like drinks and snacks to household items of various types are normal sites as they snake through cars hawking their wares. These people not only sell to commuters, they also sell to one another as the need arises. Practical trade channel and stock management happen on these streets as you see wholesalers break bulk and resell to the hawkers who re-stock periodically, based on uptake, all by the street sides.

16

These itinerant traders are synonymous with areas known with traffic bottlenecks. They migrate from location to location as traffic congestion eases off one place and moves to another. Smart sales pitches are made at motorists and commuters to generate quick sales in motion. Sometimes, the skill sets demonstrated by these sales people can make sales men in formal organizations look like rookies. While marketing and business people in formal organizations talk about the elevator pitch, these smart people do fantastic traffic motion pitches. People, in reaction to excellent sales pitches have often made unplanned purchases in traffic. Government has tried to stop these street traders, but has consistently lost the battle. Street trading has become a part of the daily reality of commuting in Lagos, and does provide some exciting variety to the boredom of cramped long drives.

Lagos has two main islands that serve as its commercial nerve centers: Lagos Island and Victoria Island. Most people who work or trade in these commercial centers live on the mainland, and so commuting between the islands and the mainland is a daily reality, especially on weekdays. Hence, to a lot of people, the Lagos traffic congestion is a way of life, especially for folks like me, who live on the mainland and work on the island. It means an average of four and a half hours of traffic every working day. When trapped in a car for four and a half hours every day, you must find a way to engage yourself. Reading, snoozing, chatting on the phone or writing are options available to you. I chose writing, and turned the traffic hours to my private time for thinking and writing. Given my very busy schedules, this book would have been practically impossible to write, but thanks to Lagos traffic, it became possible! The bulk of this book was written in the traffic. My iPad Mini is one of the best friends you can have in the traffic; big enough to enable your writing, small enough to be kept away from the view of possible traffic criminals, who may be on the prowl.

Something good indeed came out of the Lagos traffic jam!

I hope this book contributes to the practice.

PROLOGUE

This is much more than a marketing textbook. You will find anchorage in the theoretical frameworks discussed herein, but they are just to provide the intellectual setting to the practical cases in the book. Professors may disagree with the contents, because they were fashioned on the tough and dangerous battlefronts of many marketing wars, and not in the crucible of a laboratory or the safety of classroom walls.

However, if you are looking for practical and proven marketing thinking, ideas and concepts to help you succeed in your marketing career, win marketing battles, and astound your Professor, then this is your book.

INTRODUCTION

'The Meek Shall Inherit the Earth; But They'll Never Increase Market Share' -William G. McGowan

Global politics and wars are all about shareholding struggles. The focus of efforts is how much shares nations control of the world's wealth. Nations are concerned about how much share of the world territories and mineral resources like oil and gas, gold, diamond, uranium, coal, copper, etc., that they control; how much share of the world's productive force, intelligentsia, arms, agricultural produce, water, are within their power and influence; and how much share of people's minds and emotions are under their manipulations. Bitter wars are fought, won and lost for these purposes. It's a shareholding struggle.

Business and Marketing is no different. It is all about shareholding struggles. Brands and organizations go to war for shares. Mind share, Voice share, Shelf share, Wallet share, Retail presence share, Market volume and value share are all battlefields where brands struggle for supremacy. Marketing wars and battles are fought, won and lost for increase, leadership and control of shares in these various dimensions.

The introductory quote by William McGowan, the man who dared and broke AT&T's monopoly in America with MCI, captures the essence of this book. It is not a spoof of the Holy Scriptures, but a candid summary of a reality that saw him taking on a giant and going on to become America's second largest long distance carrier, and today in its transformed state, the largest communication company in the world. Meekness on the battlefield against a giant like AT&T couldn't have made this happen.

Marketing is warfare with several battles on several fronts at different times. The prize is the heart and pockets of consumers. The landscapes are the brands and product-scape. The warmongers are the marketing managers, brand managers, etc. Conference rooms and boardrooms are war rooms. In these wars, you either kill or get killed. Excuses are too costly, and so you are better off when you kill first and ask questions later. Hence, you need a killer instinct to survive the several battles and win the war. Meekness is not a virtue for the battlefield. Magnanimity in victory may be. It is not an environment for the fainthearted. Gentlemen cannot survive the terrain.

I have seen several battles and been involved in many wars in my marketing career. I have also been privileged to watch and learn from other corporate organizations' wars and battles. This singular opportunity gives me the leverage of a holistic view at the practice; and places on me the responsibility to capture the multifarious experiences for young marketers to tap into, and for growing practitioners to relish. It can also become a toolkit for anybody starting a business that requires street-smart marketing knowledge on the go.

This book is a product of over 23yrs of marketing management practice and experiences ranging from core marketing to broadcasting, Public Relations, and full advertising practice. While in advertising practice, I had very robust experiences in the business development and creative departments. From there, I moved to the advertiser's side to manage the advertising function in a multinational firm, with responsibility for the full dimensions of all marketing communication services for the company's entire portfolio of brands; and thereafter, moved into core brand management. I have since moved out of FMCG marketing into telecom services marketing, where I have had the opportunity to nurture brands from inception and became part of the team that has built the biggest brand born out of Africa.

Kill or Get killed contains examples of successes and failures; tales of battles won, battles lost and lessons learnt. There are case studies across industries from multinational FMCG companies to telecommunication and multi-sector services industries, so practicing marketers across industries can learn, adapt and adopt learning. I am hopeful that this book will add to the marketing knowledge pool amongst practitioners in Nigeria and Africa, potential market entrants in Africa and in Nigeria, and indeed practitioners globally.

CHAPTER ONE

LOGIC PLUS MAGIC

There have been debates and different schools of thought on what marketing really is. Some believe it is science, while others see it as an art. Those who see it as science focus on the data analytics, syllogism and deductive reasoning components of marketing and conclude that is all there is about marketing. The proponents of marketing as an art focus largely on the communication and consumer engagement bit of marketing, and conclude that it represents the whole. Sometimes, folks see the advertising creative process, the sponsorships and events as marketing.

Several folks from other disciplines give expressions to their desires to get into marketing, but when engaged on their understanding of the marketing concept, it becomes obvious that they saw only a couple of events hosted by the marketing division as the marketing function. A smart gentleman from another division once came to the marketing division of an organization on a job rotation. Afterwards, a few vacant positions emerged in the team due to an organizational restructuring. When he was asked if he would apply, he pointedly refused and confessed that he did not expect the level of work and intellectual rigour he met when he was coming into the division. He was very happy to return to his division. He refused to apply for any of the vacancies.

Another smart guy from an engineering background got redeployed into the Marketing division with the mindset that he was going there to have some fun. A few months down the line, he confessed that he had made very uninformed negative commentaries about marketing due to his level of ignorance about the function. In his earlier life, as far as he was concerned, marketing guys were just a bunch of smooth talking, flamboyant folks who could talk their ways through anything, but do pretty little work beyond communication, hosting events and shows, and living the fast life.

This misrepresentation is fed largely by ignorance and the fact that the closest contacts most of the folks who hold these views have with marketing folks is at marketing events. Most marketing managers are too focused on achieving numbers that they hardly have time for organizational politics, because they are driven by the passion to get the most possible number of customers to buy the most product at the most profitable price possible and at the highest frequency possible. They are therefore market and consumer focused, and not so internal customer focused as some other functions by default. This is a big minus for marketers.

However, the reality is that marketing is neither strictly science nor is it strictly art. It is a combination of both. It is a game of numbers made possible by humans. It is about delivering set financial results based on a strategic understanding, interpretation and utilization of information to produce or make a defined bundle of benefits available to a defined audience consistently at a profit better than competition can. The science of relevant information gathering, data analysis, insight generation, strategy definition, product formulation, pricing determination, etc., all reside in the realm of logic. The packaging, naming convention, branding, communication, and all other consumer engagement strategies that ensure consumers try, purchase, consistently use the product, and become advocates all reside in the realm of magic. Marketing therefore is a combination of logic and magic. It is both a science and an art. Any marketer that sees it purely from either side stands the risk of failure. An unbalanced focus on either of the two can result in disaster. You will always need the magic to sell the logic.

CHAPTER TWO

NAILING THE MOVING TARGET

Marketing starts and ends with the consumer. Excellent insights, engagement and continuous satisfaction of this consumer better than competition determine success or failure. The 21st century customer is however a peculiar specie. This consumer operates in an environment embroiled in radical changes that fundamentally affect him and that he in turn fundamentally affects. This compels continuous change of both the person and the environment. This makes this consumer a moving target in a moving world. Nailing this target demands dynamism and motion. You cannot be on one spot and expect to nail this consumer. You must keep moving after him, anticipating his needs, his whims, and accommodating his idiosyncrasies so you can satisfy and exceed his expectations at a profit.

In developing economies of the world struggling under the heavy burdens of poverty, high unemployment rate, crime, deplorable infrastructure and bad leadership, the consumer is under intense daily pressure from sunrise to sunset. Outside of the less than one percent rich, and in some cases, a small percentage of an emerging middle class, the few employed earn meager salaries that barely see them through the month due to the double demand of insufficiency and family expectations. The remaining majority are either not employed or are in menial jobs or very small scale enterprises, where they struggle continually to eke out a living.

Therefore, the mass of these customers are oppressed, depressed and difficult to please. I call them the ODD. Governments have failed them. Religion has failed them. Neighbors have failed them. They no longer trust anyone or anything. They are cynical of commercial communication, because they know it is paid for, and so the art may lack credibility.

This cynicism has not been helped by the huge onslaught of many brands competing for the customer's heart and pocket. With saturation in the European and American markets, Africa and the rest of the third world have become the focus of global brands and other regional brands from Asia. The media is under heavy bombardment with diverse commercial communications many of which are not credible. He is expected to sift through this clutter of sameness in benefits, complexity in brand names and mediocrity in communication.

Another dimension of this consumer is the impact of globalization and the digital media, especially the social media on him. The young, educated and upwardly mobile amongst them are so empowered by the digital media that they can compare the prices and claims by any brand with similar brands offering similar benefits across the globe at the click of a button. Sometimes they know much more than the marketing manager pitching to them. This category of consumers is indeed empowered to determine the fate of brands!

However, with this empowerment comes a problem; he is demanding. He knows what global standards exist and insists on it. He is brutally demanding and God help the marketing manager or company that fails to give him his demands when he wants it;

how he wants it; where he wants it, at the price he considers fair. He is not emotional. If you disappoint him, he takes his money somewhere else. He is not loyal in the way we used to view loyalty. That kind of loyalty belongs to the consumers of old, not this new generation. This consumer is loyal only to one person- himself!

This consumer is a bargain hunter who seeks for the best bargains anywhere he can get them. He is a global citizen physically resident in your neighborhood but mentally and psychologically resident in the information saturated cyberspace. He doesn't care about your local problems. He is not bothered about the impact of power problems on your cost structure and your capacity to deliver quality service. It is not his business if your ports are troubled and you have to pay double to move your input materials. He has a sense of entitlement to global standards and fair prices. Only marketers who can deliver such will be able to nail the bull's eye in terms of his attention and his money.

What worked for this customer yesterday will not work today. What works today will most likely be obsolete tomorrow. Marketers therefore need to be in a constant change mode. We must continually connect with this consumer, identify the key insights driving and changing him so we can be continually positioned to satisfy his ever-changing needs profitably.

REMEMBERING THE TITANIC

The Titanic was the largest passenger steamship in the world at the time of her launch in 1912. It had a length of 269.1 meters. It had a total capacity of 3,547 passengers, including the crew, when fully loaded. The Titanic was touted as the safest ship ever built until that time. Unfortunately, the Titanic made only one voyage. It sank on its maiden voyage two hours and forty minutes after leaving shore on the 15th of April 1912. This disaster resulted in the death of 1,517 people. It became ranked as the deadliest peacetime maritime disaster. The question is, who or what sank the Titanic? Findings show that an iceberg sank the Titanic, but what led to the mishap? The misplaced confidence of its owners, poor weather condition and the lack of caution on the part of the crew on shift that night were all said to have contributed significantly to the disaster.

Typically, only one tenth of the volume of an iceberg is above water. The shape of the remainder under the water can be difficult to predict or surmise from what is visible above the surface. The expression, 'the tip of the iceberg' originated from this fact that what is above the water is significantly smaller than what is beneath. Icebergs can be as high as 550 feet above sea level and can weigh up to 200,000 tonnes.

Customer needs are like the iceberg. What is obvious is significantly less than what lie beneath the surface of observable action. Customer needs are not just functional, emotional or a linear combination of both. There is a deeper end value aspiration underlining the functional and emotional needs. Delivering just functional and emotional benefits based on headline data from the consumer may therefore not deliver the desired results. A marketer may make the same mistake as the crew of the Titanic; to take the portion of the visible or observable need 'iceberg' as the whole to a fatal conclusion. The self-expressive need of the customer is the not so obvious desire of the consumer that normal data from traditional researches may not yield.

Demographic and psychographic researches are great, but limited in unearthing the deep underlining reasons why people think and act in certain ways, especially when it comes to trial, purchase, usage, repeat purchase and loyalty to a brand. Consumers don't just buy products. They buy into your idea or philosophy. The consumer needs to believe genuinely in your idea and brand philosophy. That is the cornerstone of an enduring relationship. Growth, loyalty and market leadership are driven by the consumer's belief in the brand's idea or philosophy.

The Brand's philosophy must be born out of a true and relevant insight. These insights in turn must be founded on beliefs and emotions, and not on behaviors. Just like the iceberg, what is obvious and easily noticeable are the behaviors. The danger is that behaviors change, so building a brand on behaviors can translate into a short life span. That brand will be a fad. It will die with the change in behavior. Emotions and beliefs, on the other hand, are more permanent. They reside beneath the surface of human actions. They represent the portion of the iceberg deep beneath the surface of the sea. They are deep seated and can alter or fundamentally change behavior, just as the iceberg can change the course of the life of a ship.

Motivational researches help to open up the consumer to understand his motivations, emotions, aspirations, values and unexpressed needs that determine behavior and attitudes. Many marketing initiatives have been disastrous just like the ill fated voyage of the Titanic, because the marketers did not understand the danger of the 90% submerged, not easily recognizable elements of the human specie that determine and alter behavior. The size of your company or marketing budget is immaterial. The Titanic was the largest ship of its time, yet it sank. The consumer is complex. You need the right tools and knowledge to get behind the veil to access insights on what drives him so you stay afloat.

CONSUMER DATA, INSIGHT AND GUTS-CAUTION NOTES TO MARKETERS

No marketer can survive or succeed without relevant and timely data. This could be easy in terms of accessing transactional data that gets generated by virtue of daily transactions in the business, or it could be a more sophisticated formal research. Data is however just data. It is of limited usage if it is not properly analyzed and understood for the insights it can yield to the trained mind. Insight is what triggers ideas or solutions to whatever brand issues that are being addressed. Some other times, insight can open up a new line of business entirely.

Data can be abused and used as a bargaining tool in the hand of mischievous managers. Data can be made to say anything depending on the context and the objective of the custodian. There have been cases where data custodians become manipulative and power drunk, because of the volume of information at their disposal and the discretion they exercise on what amount of data they release, the person they release it to, and the frequency of release.

A number of such people starve colleagues of relevant and timely information for selfish ends and practice power play at the detriment of the greater good of the business. My advice is that marketers should ensure data democracy amongst key managers who need it for planning purposes. The KPIs of the Data custodians should be structured to reward effective collaboration with the relevant departments that require the data for planning.

Never get yourself into a situation where you are at the mercy of the data custodian. It is dangerous to your professional health, the brand's health and the health of the business. A single individual should never be allowed to hold the organization to ransom. A note of caution on data: it is not absolute. It can lead to wrong assumptions and wrong decisions. This is where gut feeling borne out of experience and depth come to play. Every seasoned marketer has gut feel. This is not scientific, and may sometimes brazenly run counter to the wisdom presented by data. It should however not be discounted, because it is like the sixth sense that defies logic, but can make the difference between success and failure.

CHAPTER THREE

THOUGH IT AIN'T BROKEN, BUT MAYBE YOU SHOULD STILL FIX IT

'If it ain't broke, why fix it?' is an expression that validates the continuity of time tested principles and formulas. It surmises that as long as they work and deliver expected results, don't change them. This encourages the automation of processes and procedures based on history, but may be ill equipped to anticipate the future. The car on a race track as a metaphor for keeping an organization in a constant state of imbalance to anticipate the twists and the turns of the market race tracks may be extreme and unsettling; yet a delicate balance needs to be maintained between these two extremes.

Recent thoughts on the end of sustainable competitive advantage and the emergence of transient competitive advantage advance this position. The dynamism and speed of change that has characterized the last decade has phenomenally altered the pace of obsolescence of both strategies, products or brands, companies and even whole industries. The managers of a brand must acknowledge the place of best practices based on defined processes fashioned by analyzed history, but must build internal agility to anticipate and respond to change into its DNA such that even when it's not broken, you can still take the bold step of fixing it to own a share of the anticipated future. This requires a different mindset and a different kind of listening to the consumer.

This mindset requires marketers to continually listen to the whispers of the heart of the consumers. We need to focus not just on what they are saying audibly, but more on what they are not saying so loudly. A company that may not have done a very good job of this at a point in its history is Unilever in Kenya. Unilever historically had a firm grip on the Kenyan market within the FMCG sector. In most homes, practically everything in the kitchens and the bathrooms were from Unilever. From cooking fats to Margarine, Body soap, Detergent to Juice, most were from Unilever.

In the cooking fat category, Unilever packaged her brand in big tins that were safe and secure, but very difficult to open. Women had troubles getting the tins open with knives et al. The brand was loved, but had this packaging problem that consumers struggled with. Consumer feedback showed continually that they love the brand, but complained about the difficulty of opening the tins. However, because the complaints did not affect volume at this time, as consumers continued to purchase the brand anyway, there was no urgency to change the winning formula. Unilever therefore did nothing to change the tins.

Kapa Oil Refineries Limited observed this challenge and saw an opportunity in it. The company saw that it was possible to package cooking fats in reusable plastic containers that were easy to open and seal back; and so began to experiment with it. When the cooking fat in plastic packaging appeared in the market, Unilever did not pay much attention to it. The company was a comfortable market leader in the category with about 90% market share and didn't see any reason to change.

Kapa Oil Refineries Limited packaged a brand of cooking fat called Kasuku in easy to open plastic containers that appealed to the urban woman. When Kapa Oil Refineries Limited saw that

31

the urban woman had begun to buy Kasuku, the company developed and introduced its own brand of margarine with the same easy to open plastic packaging concept. Over a period of time, there was a shift in the urban areas from Unilever's Kimbo to the Kasuku, majorly due to the ease of opening of the packaging. At this point, Unilever still did not make a change even though the company acknowledged the market share loss in the urban areas. The consumption size in the rural areas was still significant and so the challenge from Kapa Oil Refineries Limited was not seen as life threatening. Then the easy to open Kasuku found its way into the rural areas and demand surged from both the rural and the urban areas. A big harm was done to the Unilever brand, and over time, the company lost shares on almost all her brands in the home care business, and indeed, had to sell some of her brands to Bidco, another competitor.

Today, the Kimbo brand is a Bidco brand. The company innovated around the brand and its packaging, taking it to market leadership. Unilever was left with some soaps, detergent and Blue Band. Bidco is now the market leader in the FMCG sector for home care brands in Kenya. The consumers will ultimately punish any brand that takes them for granted by migrating their consumption to competition that demonstrates it cares. Value must never be seen from the narrow perspective of the managers of the brand or the most obvious observable data. Value must be seen from a broad perspective, but especially from the well analyzed silent whispers of the consumer.

CHAPTER FOUR

IT'S AFRICA... SO WHAT?

While marketing principles are universal and global in outlook, their applications must be tempered by local knowledge and sensitivities. Thus, customization of global principles to the local African environment is critical. This requires in-depth knowledge and appreciation of the different cultures, belief systems, values, etc., of Africans to enable brands and companies connect with what Africans consider as important to them, as a prerequisite for marketing success.

WHAT'S COLOUR AND CONSISTENCY GOT TO DO WITH WINNING IN AFRICA?

Colours are very important to Africans and are connected to deep cultural interpretations and meanings that influence responses to brands and their colours or liveries. While there are usually strong responses to primary colours in Africa, some primary colours in certain categories are culturally distasteful and subliminally resisted. For instance, while black as a primary colour may evoke strength and class in certain categories like automobiles, the deep meaning of black especially amongst Anglophone Africans is death, sorrow or tragedy. Hence, if a brand chooses black as a primary colour for its logo or livery, the subliminal message it communicates may be negative. Such brands may struggle for acceptance. The same goes for brands that use colours like pink or orange. Such brands may also be subliminally perceived to be weak and struggle for acceptance.

On the other hand, black in French culture is seen as chic, classy and premium. In Anglophone Africa, it's a mixed grill. As a product colour within certain categories, it may be acceptable, but not as a brand's primary colour. A black car for instance may speak class, but a completely black dress is for mourning. Expressions of a brand with black logo or liveries may subliminally communicate gloom, sorrow and sadness; emotions that Africans would rather not be surrounded with.

Africans, especially Anglophone Africans are colorful, expressive and exuberant. Brands that will connect must give expressions to these critical dimensions of the African. Though this conclusion may not be scientific; it may, among other factors provide some explanation to some of the reasons why a brand like Orange seems to have done well in Francophone Africa, but struggles in Anglophone Africa. It may also offer some explanations to why the Zain brand struggled for acceptance in Africa.

Consistency is a critical building block for Trust. Apart from African politics where citizens have resigned to inconsistencies, Africans love consistency, and so look for it in other areas of life, like faith or brands and products, especially in categories that are not driven by impulse purchase. In certain spheres of life, it takes trauma to effect change and major dissonance with a brand to get a switch in such categories. Where the cost of switching is high, this gets even more pronounced. People hardly switch for frivolous reasons and are quick to forgive consistent brands, even when they miss it sometimes. Relationships with such brands are seen like a marriage where little misunderstandings happen, but hardly lead to divorces. Consumers at the bottom of the pyramid may change when they go bargain hunting or when economic depression forces some level of down-trading, even amongst middle income earners. Research reports often show preference for brands they consider as their first brand. A brand that is inconsistent will therefore struggle to earn the trust of Africans. Where there is no trust, patronage will be low and inconsistent. Loyalty will be a distant possibility.

In Nigeria, a telecom brand that has had to struggle with this is Airtel. The brand has had a change of ownership too many times and had evolved from Econet Wireless, to VMobile, then to Celtel, and from Celtel to Zain, before its sale to Airtel. Over these periods, the company lost the trust of the customers. This lack of trust cascaded down to the product offerings developed and marketed by the organization, and so adoption and growth was low compared to its potentials and the opportunities in the market. Though the brand has remained Airtel in the last four years, the legacy of inconsistency and the credibility question still hangs like an albatross around the neck of the brand. At the early stage of the last sale, lots of customers believed the brand would still be sold and so did not wholly trust the brand. Concerted efforts are being made by the managers of the business to effect a perception change. The nearest future will determine how far reaching these efforts are.

AFRICANS AND THE EMOTIONAL CONNECTION

The higher a product is in the value chain, the bigger the emotional connection. Cars, expensive and branded personal wares like watches, ladies' bags, men's shirts, shoes, etc., make categorical statements about the personalities of those who own them. Purchase decisions for these items are not driven by rational or logical processes, but rather by emotions. Brands like Bentley, Rolls Royce, Rolex, Gucci and Prada ladies' bags etc., are not purchased just for their functional benefits. Such is taken for granted. Rather, they are driven by what the brands say about the owners and the statements the owners are making or desire to make about themselves.

On the other hand, the lower down the value chain a product is, the more preference gets driven by a rational and logical decision making process. Here, functionality takes preeminence. Pricing and availability become key drivers of choice once the product can deliver on the basic functions.

While this may be seen as a general rule and hold true in the developed economies, there are however geographical sensitivities that temper this position. For instance, in the telecom category, choice is driven purely by logic in the developed economies. It's a function of coverage, pricing, mobile device deals, product or service offerings and customer service. This is not absolute in Africa. Emotions still play significant roles in the choice of network providers. At a point in the Kenyan telecom market, Airtel was less congested and delivered a much better experience, yet most Kenyans preferred Safaricom and would only use alternative networks in the worst of situations.

This situation was also not helped by Airtel's strategic choice to use pricing as a source of competitive advantage. Hence, consumers see the brand as a pure commodity that does not deserve loyalty and only good enough for bargain hunting. The market became conditioned to a price promotion driven brand. The brand had no deeper meaning and connection with consumers beyond price. Patronage therefore dips each time there is no price promotion.

In Europe and America where the choice of a telecom operator is purely logical and rational, price as a source of competitive advantage works. In Africa choice in the telecom category is driven by deeper motivations beyond price, and brands can be forgiven for charging a fair premium where such brands have grown to own a slice of the customers' lives or even matured to the point where it has become the asset of the market where it operates; a point where the brand is perceived as a national asset. This is what Safaricom did successfully. The brand connected deeply emotionally with Kenyans in various ways that the network became integral to the Kenyan nation.

Safaricom's introduction of Mpesa not only delivered on the functional benefit of money transfer, but also on the emotional benefit of 'Caring and Being seen to be there for loved ones' when there is the need. Historically, sending money to loved ones was fraught with a lot of frustrations and disappointments due to trust issues. It was either the monies never got delivered on time, at all or sums less than what was sent got delivered. To a teeming unbanked population, Mpesa solved this huge emotional problem, while delivering on the basic benefit of money transfer. Now, customers can be there for their loved ones when they need to. Parents back at the hinterland can get monies sent to them to meet pressing needs on time; school fees can be received on time to avoid the embarrassment of students being sent out of school for non-payment; family members can experience the loving care of their privileged ones in the city without the fear and emotional trauma of failed expectations and disappointments. Mpesa was much more than just an innovative service, it was an answer to an emotional heart cry and it transformed a commodity into an essential part of the life of the average Kenyan.

Beyond Mpesa, Safaricom made a conscious decision to make itself a champion and a promoter of Kenyan nationalism. The brand's marketing investments were focused on developing and promoting 'Proudly Kenyan' sentiments and pushed the agenda to the point of almost becoming the conscience of the nation in times of crisis. Therefore, it naturally commands a high emotional equity that translates to preference, regular usage and loyalty, despite the brand's price premium. This is a classic case of the impact of emotional equity on a brand's bottom line.

CHAPTER FIVE

DIFFERENTIATION IN THE AGE OF COMMODITIZATION

While the holy mantra of differentiate or die still holds true, commoditization of industries has made this more difficult than ever. Most organizations within industries do the same things; serve the same customers, invest in the same systems and processes, know the same things and are ignorant about the same things, recycle the same people, and deploy the same technologies. All of these mean one thing: differentiation is practically nil or has an extremely short life span!

The telecommunication industry is a perfect example here. Network technologies, both hardware and software are similar. Information technologies are similar. The same vendors supply the industry and operate account management systems for different operators, while vending the same services. Systems and processes are similar, and skilled manpower gets recycled across operators. The end results are bouquets of similar product portfolios in different names. Hence, the question of true difference and uniqueness becomes a huge challenge.

This reality extends beyond telecommunication into other categories within the service and FMCG industries. Marketing has

a Herculean task of breaking clutter and parity to achieve preference that translates to market volume and value share leadership. Three opportunities exist for the smart marketer to achieve differentiation. These include:
*Go To Market strategy,
*Route To Market strategy
*Excellent customer care.

You can be differentiated in how you take the proposition to the market to achieve immediate presence and impact, trial and brand endearment. Your creativity is your only limitation. The same goes for the route to market. You can change the game fundamentally by your route to market strategy, and of course, the innovativeness and genuineness of your customer care strategy.

DIFFERENTIATED MARKET ENTRY:
THE GLOBACOM PER SECOND BILLING CASE

Within the Nigerian telecommunication sector, Globacom's entry strategy at launch was very disruptive and differentiated. Before the brand launched, the entire industry billed customers per minute based on global standard and practice. However, the brand needed to turn its late entrance into an advantage. It did this via its Go To Market strategy.

It leveraged on nationalistic sentiments as the only truly Nigerian brand within the telecommunication space validated by a populist stance as the people's champion. It introduced the Per second billing, used iconic Nigerians and opinion leaders as endorsers and encouraged Nigerians in its payoff to exude national pride with the 'glow with pride' rallying cry and the use of the national colors. It was a 'For Us By Us' strategy that got a significant segment of Nigerian consumers excited that a 'saviour' had arrived at last to deliver them from perceived imperialist brands. The brand got an immediate break into the market, endeared itself to Nigerians and turned the people against the incumbent networks for earlier claims that it was impossible to bill per second at that stage of the industry's lifecycle.

Sample of Glo Per second billing advertising

The second differentiation opportunity is in Route To Market. A brand that exemplified the effectiveness of this strategy and changed the Nigerian retail landscape is Promasidor.

REDEFINING RETAIL TRADE, MERCHANDISING AND BRAND VISIBILITY IN NIGERIA: THE PROMASIDOR COWBELL MILK CASE

Promasidor, formerly known as Wonder Foods, redefined retail trade, merchandising, and brand visibility in Nigeria with Cowbell Milk. Before this time, no company had sold milk in any repacked form in the open market. Cowbell saw an opportunity in a trade practice and imported 25kg bags of Cowbell Milk, sold them in the open market, where bulk breakers opened them up and sold in measures to retailers who in turn scooped them into very small sizes for sale to consumers at very affordable price points. Despite the health hazards associated with this retailing model, sales boomed and the company was encouraged to push the frontiers.

5,10 and 15 gram pack sizes were nonexistent within the cocoa based beverage and dairy milk industry before the advent of Cow-bell milk. However, the economy was at a downturn. Inflation had eroded the value of the meager disposable income for those who could still earn. Consumers were trading down, and small pack sizes allowed them to manage the issue of outlay. Cowbell was a lifesaver to this group of consumers! The brand brought in these small pack sizes and sales grew phenomenally. Immediate response by the existing category leaders was difficult. Invest-ments in machinery and a change of business model were re-quired. These fundamentals couldn't happen overnight. Market share was lost to this challenger brand.

Promasidor also changed the marketing industry's attitude to route to market, merchandising, and brand visibility. The com-pany did not just settle for the standard distribution strategy, but went beyond the traditional, to close the commercial last mile, the retailers. Promasidor created an effective system and struc-ture that ensured retail presence even in the most remote areas in Nigeria.

The retail channels were well delineated and stocked. Retailer ki-osks were deployed and frequently visited by the sales team. The outlets were heavily branded and merchandising materials were generously given out to the retailers. With time, the landscape was adorned in the brand's blue and white colors. They were so bold and strong, such that no one could miss them. They heralded a new era of cheaper, easy to deploy brand merchandising and vis-ibility. Even though the environment was adversely affected, and the government eventually had to regulate brand merchandising, but the brand had gotten the much-needed break it desired into the Nigerian market.

(More detailed case on Promasidor in the Milk war in later portions of the book)

The advent of online stores and retail chains in Nigeria and other parts of Africa are opening up new opportunities in the retail environment. Brands now have more options and are better positioned to close the commercial last mile more successfully than before. As the chains and the online stores grow, purchase patterns will change, and the traditional distribution structures may eventually give way. This will start off a new type of war amongst brands in-store.

The third differentiation opportunity in a commoditized industry is the excellent customer care platform. This goes beyond the tangible benefits of what the brand or proposition does to how the proposition makes the customer feel at the point of engagement and during disaster recovery. This is especially critical within the service industry. How you make the customer feel can obliterate the negatives of premium pricing and create advocates. All men love to be treated like kings even though many people originate off low estates.

Brands can come back from the brink of a disaster to win a customer back and turn such a customer to an advocate, depending on its customer care strategy. How far a brand is willing to go to redress a fault in its offering or customer experience can make a huge difference in its perception. This is different from a proactive retention strategy that rewards customers for continued patronage or loyalty. This type takes the delivery of the basic service paid for by the customer for granted. It is over and above the customer's basic expectations.

The success of any or all of these strategies depends on the robustness and competitiveness of the core product or value proposition. If the core proposition is defective, none of the strategies can work. Such a scenario can be likened to a seated beautiful lady with a deformed bone structure. Her deformity prevents her from standing even though she is a gorgeous beauty. We can get leading world designers to make and dress her up. The moment of truth is when an unsuspecting admirer asks her for a dance or asks to walk her down the aisle. His affections may most likely fade off instantly at the discovery of her disability. If a brand cannot or does not deliver on the core brand promise consistently, it has broken trust and it is a matter of time before such a brand becomes history. You cannot afford to take the consumer for a ride. He'll make you pay dearly.

CHAPTER SIX

THE VALUE PROPOSITION QUESTION

A sound understanding of the consumer is not just an academic exercise. The intention is to develop the right value proposition package that will best meet the identified needs of the consumer, presented in the right way at the right price and at an easy reach to the consumer.

The Value Proposition package is therefore developed to deliver the benefits that insights into the consumer's needs have yielded. These benefits are threefold and they answer three fundamental questions. They are Functional, Emotional and Self-expressive.

Functional benefits deal with what the value proposition does for the consumer. It answers the question, **what does it do for me functionally?** If it is a wristwatch and it is meant to indicate time to the consumer, does it deliver on that? Does it do it well effectively and efficiently?

The emotional benefit focuses on answering the question, '**how does it make me feel?** Still using the wristwatch as an example, is its accuracy such that I can trust it and each time I tell anybody what time it is by my watch, or plan my schedules based on it, is it always accurate? If this watch is an expensive well recognized designer watch and not a cheap and cheerful unbranded watch, how does it make me feel when I wear it? Do I feel emotionally fulfilled to know that it confers on me some level of social acceptance amongst my peers? Such kinds of watches that deliver on emotional benefits can make the customer wear short sleeve shirts!

The third question is, 'what does it say about me?' A high-end Rolex wristwatch, a Bentley, and/or a Porsche Panamera, definitely speak volumes about their owners or users. Even if the customer had borrowed the Porsche, being seen to have driven the car into a function immediately creates an image in the mind of onlookers and other guests that the driver or owner is a person of style and substance. A compelling value proposition must say something about its user or owner. If it says something contrary to the belief, motivations, and emotions of the user, it has failed.

The value proposition package defines the extent of the relevance of a brand to its target customer. It establishes a credible platform for the brand to communicate its reason for being or point of view. A compelling and relevant value proposition package is what successful brands are built upon. It is the tangible expression of the brand promise. Apart from sound consumer insight as the bedrock of a relevant and compelling value proposition package, there is also the competitive context that must be considered. You do not operate as an island. Your strategy must be contextual. It must factor in your competi-

A compelling and relevant value proposition package is what successful brands are built upon

tive terrain. It must anticipate competition's strategies and develop tactical interventions to ward off aggression, while focusing on own strategy.

GO TO MARKET STRATEGY

A contextual macro-environmental scan is important as the prelude to a good Go To market Strategy document. It sets the tone for an appropriate understanding of the issues and the environment that the proposition is about to be birthed into. Issues about the political environment, economic context, social environment, technological dynamics, environmental issues, especially within the ecological context and the current focus on global warming, in addition to the Legal environment and how it may affect the product's performance are analyzed for implications. The output of this exercise helps the marketer to screen the proposition for its competitive value creation and delivery potentials.

Often, young marketers confuse the Go To Market strategy with the brand's communication strategy. This is a very narrow way of looking at this. Marketers desirous of winning the war must think commercially; in which case, not only should the Go To Market strategy look at the historical marketing mix of the 4Ps: Product, Pricing, Place, and Promotion, it should also look at newer dimensions of the commercial mix, including the customer experience and corporate social responsibility dimensions.

The value proposition is not just the basic product. It is a bundle of benefits made up of the core product, its presentation, packaging, pricing and the different expressions of the brand's philosophy beyond the basic benefits. These are covered under the first two historical Ps: Product and Pricing. This is where the Go To Market strategy begins. Once you have resolved the first two Ps, you now need to ensure an impactful market entry. This requires commercial thinking. You need to determine your Sales and Distribution structure that will ensure availability at every point of purchase; dealer commission structure, systems and processes to determine the most optimal route to market that will ensure immediate impact and achieve the desired objectives. You cannot do this alone. You need your Sales and Distribution counterpart, a step in the commercial direction.

To close the commercial loop before discussing the Promotions mix that has taken on variegated meanings and dimensions in the last couple of years, an element that is becoming increasingly important in the highly competitive landscape is customer experience. Historically, customer relations as it was called for a long time was seen as a disaster recovery role and paid minimal attention in the development of marketing strategies. However, this role has become more proactive than ever, especially in the service industry. Now you can generate trial, up sell, deep sell, cross sell, engage and reward your customers with the technological advancements recorded over the last ten years in the customer experience or customer care discipline. Your commercial Go To Market strategy is therefore incomplete until this element is integrated.

The Promotions mix is the last leg of the Go To Market strategy and it focuses on the marketing communication dimensions of how you take the value proposition package to the market. We've seen significant evolutions and breakthrough thinking in this area. For instance, the advertising landscape has significantly evolved with the change in mode of consumption of marketing communication by targets. The 360-degree wheel of total communication has been enhanced to include digital marketing, digital communication and mobile marketing. Sponsorships and Events have also taken on greater importance and significance in the last couple of years, driven on one hand by steep media cost increments, and on another hand by the tobacco and alcoholic beverage categories. Regulations restrict these categories from engaging in normal marketing communications campaigns at prime time and on certain media formats. Significant percentages of brand budgets have therefore been diverted into Sponsorship and Events activations.

The advent of YouTube, the largest TV channel in the world, Mobile TV and Internet TV has also redefined the TV format. Hence, planning for TV requires a different mindset from production to exposure. The days of passive TV consumption are gone. Today's customer wants to be involved, even in the way you develop the communication you want to expose him to and how you share it with him. Apart from the awesome power of the remote control, there is also the absolute power of the mouse.

> **The days of passive TV consumption are gone. Today's customer wants to be involved, even in the way you develop the communication you want to expose him to and how you share it with him.**

The Print format has not been spared either. Digital media has grown to a point where the old matrix for measuring newspaper circulation is fast becoming obsolete. Digital eyeballs as a metric is gaining currency, because a lot of newspapers now publish online versions that deliver wider readership across geographies and demographics than physical prints do. Advertising materials also get reproduced faithfully on such editions. The Nigerian marketing and marketing communication industry's pursuit of the establishment of the Audit Bureau of Circulation in Nigeria has had to be reevaluated in the light of this development.

Other elements of the Promotions mix like the Radio is also undergoing changes. In Nigeria, consumers listen more to the radio on their mobile devices than they do on traditional devices like transistors. Internet radio is also growing and may soon take on significant importance. The outdoor industry is not left out of the waves of change too. It is also changing rapidly from format to size, electronic to digital, lease tenor to message mix.

The boom in the Sponsorship and Events industry is raising the issue of impact measurement and returns on investment. The more money the sector gets allocated, the greater the demand for results. Globally, the question is being asked; beyond the age long stereotype answer of affinity and brand equity, what else can a sponsorship property deliver? This is a new field of research and development now. Measurement models with scientific formulas are being developed daily to make sense of the intangible impact of sponsorship properties. Marketers must plan with all these re-alities; capture them in the Go To Market strategy and budget for them.

CHAPTER SEVEN

ON COMPETITION... DON'T PRESS THE PANIC BUTTON YET!

I hate panic. I have had to deal with panic moments at different times in my career. It never ceases to amaze me how organizations fly into the panic mode once competition does anything that attracts market attention. My view is that my competitors were also smart enough to hire brilliant people to work in their marketing and business development divisions. They have access to rich data and insights for developing compelling propositions; they have shareholders who demand the most optimal returns for their investment and a board committed to doing the same. It is, therefore, unrealistic to expect these brilliant minds to go to sleep while we work.

I am also of the view that marketing is warfare made up of many battles. The loss of a battle does not mean the loss of the war, as long as you don't lose the strategic battles that define the war. Be careful that panic does not become an integral feature of your operational module. There was an organization that used to hit the panic button every time its main competitor's report got published. Managers of the business were subjected to the pressure immediately. Numbers were revised and a maniacal drive to beat the numbers from competition started. It took a long time before the organization discovered that a category it was not competing in was responsible for the numbers the competitor was posting.

From my perspective, if you stay on top of your game in terms of accurate consumer insight; sound, robust and relevant value proposition development; excellent go to market strategy; efficient route to market; adaptive and flexible organizational agility to exploit and ride the waves of market opportunities and changes, all effectively communicated better than competition, you may lose some battles, but you are in good stead to win the war.

When your competitor does something brilliant, be honest enough to acknowledge it to yourself. Don't get conceited and get into the mindset of condemning it out of pride. Analyze it for its brilliance and its impact on your own proposition and the market, especially in the arena of the hearts and minds of consumers. Then, devise a response strategy or tactic to cage its impact. Point to note here is that it is not compulsory that your response must be totally different. Sometimes, it is more strategic to respond with a copy of what the competitor has done. It's a function of context.

Sometimes, while conceptualizing ideas to respond to competitive action, silly pride by Marketing Managers and Directors has led to wastage. Discounts the consumers did not ask for get thrown at them. Value gets

When your competitor does something brilliant, be honest enough to acknowledge it to yourself. Don't get conceited and get into the mindset of condemning it out of pride.

destroyed and the entire industry suffers, as brands struggle to outdo one another. At other times,a delayed response or no response might be more strategic, especially if you are dealing with either a crafty competitor or a competitor with very limited scruples. Such competitors can lead you into a trap. Context, a good understanding of market dynamics and the character of the competitor are very critical. Excellent scenario planning and war simulation, even in the time of peace, helps to deal with the realities when they occur. Learn to expect considerable levels of insanities and think through a containment plan. If no disruption occurs, enjoy your peace, but be in a nimble and ready mode in the event one occurs.

A lot of knee-jerk reactions happen when panic steps in. You may end up leaving money on the table when the customer is not asking for it, or embarking on an investment of very limited value with your limited resources. The golden rule is not to get into analysis overdrive or paralysis, while your market share disappears. Prepare for war in the time of peace. When the war does come, its mode may be different, but you are not totally caught off guard. Not to respond on time when you need to is suicide. Responding too early could also be wastage. Embrace analytics. It is good, but give room for your guts too based on the context. No marketer gets far without it.

Embrace analytics. It is good, but give room for your guts too based on the context. No marketer gets far without it.

Competition is good when it is rational. It drives strategic and operational excellence. It becomes value destroying when you have to deal with an irrational competitor who may also enjoy some scale economics you do not have. At this point, you need to change the rules of the game. You need to redefine the competitive landscape. Change the battle terrain. Price as a tool for competitive advantage will bleed you to death. Explore other frontiers for differentiation.

CHAPTER EIGHT

HERE COMES THE CHALLENGERS: NEW BATTLES, NEW WARS, UNUSUAL STRATEGIES

Some brands have enjoyed near monopolies for several years and have grown to become mega brands or clear market leaders in their categories. The marketing organizations behind these brands embrace continuous investments in thought leadership as the driver for market leadership, and to make attempts at any direct challenge of such brands sound insane. These are the kinds of brands that Challenger brands take on. To the risk-averse brand manager, this is absolute insanity. Edgy, risk taking, irreverent, irritating, and sometimes downright crazy; these adjectives describe Challenger brands, their managers and their attitude to market leaders, competition and winning. These brands challenge the norm, redefine the competitive landscape and change the rules of war.

In the exercise of their strategic insanities, some of these brands have grown where they were not given a chance of survival; displaced market leaders in certain circumstances by innovating an entire value chain; have developed new markets and grown categories beyond where the traditional competitors had pegged growth. These were done by challenging the reigning norms and rethinking the product in the category, the packaging form and format, the pricing, the distribution, the communication, and most critically, the consumer. These were backed up with bold actions and execution excellence. Traditional competitors have been hurt. Market leaders have been bruised and market equilibriums have been disrupted.

The following cases illustrate how these brands operate, and possible lessons.

THE MILK WAR: PROMASIDOR'S COWBELL VERSUS WAMCO'S PEAK MILK

From the late eighties into the early 90s, Nigeria saw the end of the oil boom and reduced earnings by the government. Given the fact that the proceeds from the boom were not well invested, there was an immediacy of impact on the lives of the common man negatively. The exchange rate depreciated, the economy declined and poverty grew. Infrastructure decay got worse and real per capita private consumption fell. Consumers traded down from premium brands to value brands, and purchase patterns changed significantly from bulk buying to smaller pack sizes, to manage outlay based on the shriveling disposable income.

Wonder Foods Nigeria Limited emerged in this economic landscape in 1992. The company began the importation of a brand of milk called Cowbell into Nigeria, starting with the 400Gram pack size. This particular pack size did not quite succeed, because it had serious competition from other brands, especially the market leader, Peak. The company then focused on the importation of the 25kg bag. The market broke this pack and began to scoop the powder milk into transparent polythene bags to resell in very small pack sizes. The company saw a huge opportunity in the small pack size invention by the trade, and started importing small pack sizes.

However, the company had a challenge with distribution, because the existing distribution structure used by the multinationals at this point refused to stock or distribute the product. The traditional structure did not give the company and the brand the chance to survive. The team was then forced to invent its own channel structure. It turned to retailers with special emphasis on 'Mallam Tables'. These were ubiquitous structures very popular for retail sales around residential areas, schools, and market places. The company commissioned AC Nielsen to provide her with data on the total universe of the 'Mallam Tables' in Nigeria. Armed with this knowledge, the company delineated the universe and mandated her staff to visit every Mallam Table to sell just one 7.5 gram sachet. Selling to the whole universe meant selling about 15,000 sachets. The company proceeded to merchandise the table with a 'Sold Here' sign. Soon after this, the Mallams began to demand for more, and the company seized the opportunity to scientifically delineate routes and efficiently planned the itineraries of the sales teams to maximize the sales opportunities. Each member of the sales force was mandated to develop close relationships with the Mallams and know the names of every contact on each itinerary. They knew the Mallams and their routines; when they opened and when they closed so there were no wasted calls.

One of the company's major challenges was capital to invest behind the brand to manage her marketing and cost of sales. The sales team did not have vehicles for distribution, and so the challenge of moving stocks arose as demand increased. To solve this problem, the company turned to a religious sect known for its itinerant nature and the selling skills of its adherents; the Jehovah Witness religious group. Members of this group are trained to do door to door evangelism and sales of their literature, which they carry on them. Recruitment of staff into the company's sales team was therefore, focused on this group, and members enthusiastically responded and became the core of the sales team.

Given this focus and the economic condition at this time, sales boomed as the mass of Nigerians saw in Cowbell, an opportunity to still drink milk in an environment where cost had made the existing brands prohibitive. The company's financial fortune improved slightly and she began to invest in vehicles for the sales team. Nevertheless, marketing spend to build the brand was still a challenge, and so the company had to turn the vehicles into 'Moving Media' with heavy branding in Cowbell brand name, logo and livery. At this point, there were no strict rules on mobile truck or vehicle advertising in the country, it was free. These trucks were used to move stock into the semi urban and rural areas on specific market days where rural people who had never seen the Cowbell product before were educated, sampled and sold to. The converted retailers soon began to demand for the product from their own distributors in the urban and semi urban areas. These were the traditional distributors who had shunned Cowbell earlier and refused to stock or sell. Suddenly, they saw a reversal of the old order. Demand pull was leading the push. The retailers' demand for the product forced them to rescind their earlier decision not to stock or distribute Cowbell. The table turned and the distributors went looking for the company. The company, however, insisted on doing business with these distributors differently. There were no credit sales, unlike what was then the norm. It was cash sales popularly called, 'cash and carry'.

Demand grew despite this rule, and with it came the problem of cash handling. The company was subsequently forced to approach MDS, a traditional distribution company with over forty branches across the country, to manage the cash handling. The traditional channels were making huge demands that the company struggled to meet. This gave birth to a new set of problems: huge stock pile with the risk of expiration, which in turn led to a new invention: the redistribution structure. The company pulled back her sales team and refocused them to do re-distribution. They were equipped with trucks, cars, and even bicycles, and attached to distributors. Their job was to pick stock from the distributor, go into the hinterlands to sell the stock and remit both the profit and capital back to the distributor. On the back of the initial semi-urban and rural penetration, education, sampling and sales that had been done, this was a roaring success. The product's distribution grew in width and depth. Market share grew. The distributors were happy. The company became financially stronger and more successful.

With an improved financial status, the company was now in a good stead to invest behind the marketing of the Cowbell brand. In spite of this, the marketing spend was still not enough to take on the big brand in the category, so the company chose to invest differently. Tin plates that had been used and dropped by other brands were developed in large quantities and posted not only on the Mallams' Tables, but also on every available space across the country. The messages were simple and the colors were very strong and visible. Walls were painted and the cartoon character on the pack was animated to produce TV commercials. The communication and marketing efforts were focused on the emerging milk drinkers and not on the traditional consumers who were loyalists of Peak, the market leader then. Children in the lower middle class and the mass market were Cowbell's target, and so marketing investments were strategically focused on growing this base of milk drinkers. It was the milk for the people. Huge volume was the target. These categories of people were content to have something that colored their tea and gave a milky look and feel. Brand premiumness ranked nil on their priority.

Merchandising investments followed the same pattern. While other brands made expensive, but few merchandise, the company invested in huge volumes of cheap and cheerful merchandise, and filled the environment with well branded merchandise like T-shirts and baseball caps that other premium brands would have considered as sub-standard, but which the core target was happy to own and wear.

A major milk manufacturer and market leader bore the brunt of the Promasidor attack on the market the most, due to a conspiracy of factors. The company was then called WAMCO (West African Milk Company), the manufacturers of Peak Milk and Three Crowns Milk. This company was not equipped to respond with a sachet packaging option, which required new machinery, and so could not immediately compete on pack size and price points. The company's flagship and cash cow was the Peak evaporated milk in Can. The downturn in the economy had forced a lot of down-trading and loss in market share. The epileptic state of power supply added to the problems, because most consumers were compelled to finish each can opened due to inabilities to refrigerate for preservation. Cowbell on the other hand was powder and in sachet that could be opened, tied back for preservation and still fit for consumption afterwards. Thus, Promasidor had a field day eating away at WAMCO's market share. The company pursued a strategy aimed at replacing the word 'Milk' with 'Cowbell', and utilized every available means and material to do so. Company staff wore Cowbell branded uniforms. Each had fourteen shirts and fourteen pairs of trousers. Cheap T-shirts and Face caps were given in abundance. Home appliances including wares like Mugs, Fans and buckets in the homes of members of staff were Cowbell branded. Hence, each member of staff was an excited ambassador preaching the gospel of turning Cowbell into the generic reference for milk.

A brand persona and identity was designed for the Cowbell brand as 'Trendy, Intelligent and Fun loving'. To give credence to the 'Intelligence' persona, the company began the sponsorship of the Cowbell Mathematics Competition amongst secondary schools in Nigeria. This national competition gave the company a huge opportunity to recruit new users via free dry and wet sampling amongst several thousands of students. In addition to this, strong emotional connections were generated with the students through the free branded educational and personal item merchandise that were abundantly given to the students. Schools Inter-house sports events were another platform that Cowbell invested in to achieve her new users' recruitment targets. These were low cost, but effective investments that yielded good results and grew trial, adoption, regular usage and ultimately grew the brand's market share. The brand's marketing communication had also been enhanced with increased prosperity. Exciting animated TV commercials that appealed to children built on the platform; 'Cowbell, Our Milk' were developed and given good airplay. Other traditional media like the outdoor and radio media were utilized. Cowbell soon became a household name and one of the most visually recognized brands in the country.

WAMCO was ill prepared for an effective counter attack to arrest its market share loss and regain market leadership. It finally did with a two-pronged attack. A major volume driver for Promasidor's Cowbell milk then was the 400 Gram Can pack size. WAMCO targeted this pack size in her response. The company had always had a 400 Gram can pack size, which was expensive. It however decided to introduce this same 400 Gram pack size in the less expensive sachet format. This was then priced at the same price point as the Cowbell 400 Gram can. The savings on packaging was transferred to the consumer. This strategy was aimed at addressing three key issues: the competitiveness of the price point, the refrigeration challenge and volume push to regain market share loss. The company also decided to import the 25kg pack size of her low premium brand, Three Crowns Milk, to compete with the Cowbell 25kg bags that retailers repack in the open market. Very exciting marketing communication campaigns were then developed and given effective airplay to demonstrate the Peak 400 gram sachet value, reinforce the premiumness of the Peak brand, and communicate the superior value of Three Crowns milk within its segment.

This strategy met with limited success. Peak milk had a robust reputation as the 'peak of the pack' and so was aspirational for a lot of consumers. A 400gram pack size of Peak Milk at the same price point as Cowbell with a lower profile was designed to make

Cowbell unattractive. Consumers that traded down because of the downturn in the economy found a reason to return to their favorite brand at the new affordable price point. They were however small in number compared to the larger newly cultivated group of milk drinkers that Cowbell appealed to. At this point, this group was about twenty four million youngsters. They represented the new market and the market of the future for Cowbell. Even though Three Crowns Milk had a slightly more positive image than Cowbell and was attractive to consumers at the low end of the market, the volume throughput still could not match Promasidor's Cowbell's. Peak milk also struggled with the grey market influx of the imported version of the brand. The packaging for the imported version was the same as the one made by WAMCO, but more attractive. Consumers perceived the imported one as superior to the Nigerian Peak milk, and so volume suffered too. Hence, the brand was fighting internal battles, Cowbell, and several other brands that flooded the market at this period. It was a difficult place for the brand to be.

FINDING NEW USES AND NEW USERS

Apart from developing new users of Cowbell, Promasidor also developed new uses for the Cowbell milk. These new categories of users were huge volume movers. They were Confectioners, Bakers and Yoghurt makers. This group used the brand as intermediate products and raw materials for their own products. Single purchases were as much as 100 25kg sacks of Cowbell representing several days of sales by competition. The company developed a scheme where people were sent to learn how to make Yoghurt so they can teach others to expand the market for milk sales to Yoghurt makers. In addition to this, the company used a substantial portion of the milk as raw materials into developing other product lines, like Cowbell Chocolate flavor. At this point in history, there were about 72 milk brands in the market. Cowbell had a whopping 38% share of this market. Despite this convolution, the

OUR MILK

OUR MILK...
Always

Samples of Cowbell
Advertising and
Sponsorship

2013 COWBELL
NATIONAL SECONDARY SCHOOLS
MATHEMATICS COMPETITION

Approved by Federal Ministry of Education

STAR PRIZE

The National Champions and their Mathematics Teachers in both senior and junior categories will be sponsored to an all expenses paid vacation.

PRIZES FOR WINNING SCHOOLS

1st Prize:
5 Desktop Computers and Printers

2nd Prize:
3 Desktop Computers and Printers

3rd Prize:
1 Desktop Computer and Printer

HOW TO ENTER

The competition is open to students from 10-18 years of age attending private and public Secondary Schools full time in Nigeria. Entry into this competition is FREE. Only the BEST 6 (SIX) students in Mathematics – 3 from JSS3 and 3 from SSS2 (irrespective of sex, religion or state of origin) from each school are eligible to sit for this examination.

Each School head should collect 6 (SIX) registration forms, which must be correctly filled, stamped and signed by the School Principal and presented by the Students to the officials at the examination centre on the examination day. School Principals may also download registration forms online at www.promasidor-ng.com.

NATIONAL PRIZES

(A) Junior Category		(B) Senior Category
N250,000	1st	N300,000
N200,000	2nd	N250,000
N150,000	3rd	N200,000

The top 10 students in the senior category at the national level will also receive laptops.

STATE PRIZES

(A) Junior Category		(B) Senior Category
N25,000	1st	N25,000
N20,000	2nd	N20,000
N15,000	3rd	N15,000

OTHER PRIZES

• BENSON OWEKA'S MEMORIAL PRIZE: Higher Education Exercise Books & Pens for all the Students of the Winning School. This prize goes to the School with the most consistent and outstanding performance average over a three-year period.

For this year, we are looking at the period 2011 – 2013.

• N15, 000 each as consolation prizes for 14 candidates and lots of Cowbell Products

• Cash awards to mathematics teachers of winning candidates at both state and national levels

• Trophies, plaques, mathematical sets, medals, certificates, T-shirts, Face caps, stationery kits and more

• Mathematics textbooks and high class metal signposts for the top 3 schools in each category

EXAMINATION DATE

Saturday, 16 March 2013. 10:00am Prompt (Accreditation of candidates begins at 8:00am)

Candidates are advised to check their results online at www.promasidor-ng.com as from Wednesday, 22 May 2013. Please refer to the list of examination centres to confirm the location of the centre nearest you.
For more information please call: 01-7409557, 01-9504789, Blessing on 08053013526, Niyi on 08023007833 or Omonigho on 08035679595

COWBELL 20 YEARS
Nourishing Dreams

brand won the milk war, not just by differentiating and innovating on different fronts within the traditional commercial ecosystem, but by also developing new uses and expanding the universe of milk drinkers via the cultivation of new users.

THE WAR OF THE STOUTS: LEGEND EXTRA STOUT VERSUS GUINNESS FES

The Nigerian Beer market is divided into two broad categories: the Lager and the Stout. The malt drink, which is a by-product of the brewing process, is a third category and battlefield amongst the brewing giants in Nigeria. The Lager is the biggest in volume size. Malt drinks and stout vary in volume size leadership, depending on time and the strategic roles the companies want them to play per period. Despite Lager's volume leadership, the Stout remained the most profitable per hectoliter by far. This market was dominated for so long by one company and one brand, Guinness FES. Nigerian Breweries, now Heineken led the Lager and Malt categories.

Nigerian Breweries did a strategic review of her position and concluded that it was unhealthy and potentially dangerous for the company to leave Guinness alone in the extremely profitable Stout category. The company's leadership was concerned that Guinness could become so wealthy from the lucrative and highly profitable stout market to a point where it could choose to fight her on the Lager and Malt fronts. A decision was therefore taken to compete against Guinness in the Stout category. This decision was reinforced by the fact that Heineken International was not completely new to the Stout category. Murphy's Milk Stout in Ireland is a Heineken brand. Hence, the terrain that Nigerian Breweries had chosen to tread was not totally strange to the parent company, but very new to the Nigerian subsidiary.

Various researches were conducted with Guinness consumers,

and feedbacks indicated that some consumers were dissatis-
fied with Guinness and were yearning for an alternative. These
consumers believed the brand was very expensive, but also felt
trapped, because there were no alternatives. They were eagerly
looking forward to a 'saviour' brand that would open the prison
doors. Extensive researches were done during the product development process until the company felt it had the winning formula.
With this confidence, the company launched Legend Extra Stout
with a big bang in 1992. The launch was very big and it generated
a lot of positive word of mouth within the marketing community in Nigeria. The response to the launch was good. Deliberately
priced to be about twenty percent cheaper than Guinness FES,
consumer trial was huge. They were however very disappointed
because the experience was not what they had envisaged. The
product was not exactly ready to deliver on the taste experience
consumers were looking for. The company had acted too hastily
with devastating consequences. The brand had been launched in
a big way. Consumers had responded in a big way, tried it in a big
way and got disappointed in a big way. As a result, Legend Extra
Stout had a big problem.

The company went back to the drawing board and began a process
of refining the product to correct the initial challenges and deliver
on the experience and taste expectations of the consumers. When
the company finally believed it had the right product, several
blind tests were conducted with the new product and Guinness
Stout. The result of the blind tests showed that in several markets
where the research was conducted, consumers preferred Legend
Extra Stout. However, the moment the product was bottled and
put on the shelf, consumers rejected it because of the negative
memories of the initial experience. This negative perception in a
market ruled by the larger-than-life image of the Guinness brand
made breaking into the Stout market more difficult for Legend.
In an environment where Guinness was the generic reference for
Stout in the Nigerian Beer market, and the only memory of an as-
piring competitor was negative, the future looked more assured

than ever for Guinness, and more uncertain for the Challenger.

However, the company was confident of the new product and believed that if consumers could only be persuaded to try the product, they would realize that it was a better product than the initial one launched, and also a more competitive product within the stout category. Decisions to switch could then follow. At this point, management was not comfortable with any heavy financial investment in marketing the brand, because its future was not sure yet, in addition to the fact that such investments may be reinforcing the negative hangover of the initial experience. Consequently, the brand could not engage in the traditional mode of marketing communications for re-launch. Inducing consumer trial through other means was therefore critical to the success of the new product. This gave birth to the Legend Hot Spots.

The brand piloted the Legend Hot Spots scheme in Lagos and Benin, where large shops with high traffic were selected and smart sales promotion agents were recruited and stationed permanently with the shops like permanent staff. They resumed and closed with the bars, and their jobs were to promote Legend, engage in mass sampling to generate trial and push sales. This campaign was themed, 'Express Yourself', and it was meant to create a liberation experience for consumers from the prison of the market leader. Consumer feedback was sought and the reports indicated positive shocks from consumers that the brand tasted better than the initial experience. With this, acceptance began to grow, but was not universal across bars. Bars where the promoters were not present still refused to stock. Hence, the challenge the managers of the brand had to deal with at this point was getting all the bars to stock the brand. This understanding energized the company to consider further investment behind the brand, not in the traditional marketing communication channels still, but in distribution. A strategic focus was put on distribution to ensure the brand's presence at every consumption point such that if trials were generated, availability could complement the efforts. The distribution channels were incentivized and focus was on a flank-ing strategy at the regions. The trade embraced the brand in the regions and demand surged.

The growth in support from the trade, stocking and consumer demand boosted the morale of the managers of the brand and a decision was taken to enhance the brand via a label change. This was low budget as the main cost was the cost of changing the cylinder. There was still no traditional marketing communication support; but the positive impact of this label change was huge and demand surged further. Distributors began to form their own Legend Clubs and some even opted to be exclusive distributors of the brand, which meant they were no longer stocking compe-tition. At this point, the brand managers believed they could be even more adventurous, and so took the marketing and distribu-tion beyond the regions and went national. A bottle change idea was also mooted, approved and implemented. The launch of the new bottle fundamentally changed the fortune of the brand. At this point, some investments were made in traditional advertising with radio spots and outdoor hoardings. The TV spot was very tactical and focused only on the computer-generated image of the liquid to show its richness. No big TV advertising was shot!

Demand however grew significantly to a point where the com-pany could not meet volume expectations, and for the first time in the history of any brand in Nigeria, the brand had to run an advertising campaign to apologize to her loyal and prospective consumers that it was sold out! The brand however promised to be back with sufficient volume to take care of market demands, because as at the moment, investment decisions had been made to expand production capacity. Today, the brand commands over twenty percent of the stout market in Nigeria from a histori-cal paltry 3 percent. The market leader, Guinness Foreign Extra Stout lost market share to this challenger. This battle had been long drawn and was a marathon, not a sprint.

We Are Working Hard To Meet Your Demand

We wish to apologize to our numerous consumers who have been unable to get Legend Extra Stout in the quantity they want. This has been due to the unprecedented demand, (following the re-launch) which has stretched our capacity.

We are working very hard to expand capacity and produce enough to meet the ever-fast growing demand for the brand in the shortest possible time.

We thank you for your loyal support and assure that very soon, you will get enough of the real deal.

Legend, the real deal.

18+
Drink Responsibly

Sample Ad of the Legend Sold Out campaign

Worthy of note is that the Legend brand successfully challenged the age long marketing notion that you need the full complement of the traditional marketing communication tools to build a brand successfully. Depending on the category, getting the product right, the pricing right, and the distribution right, combined with creative consumer engagement initiatives can and do work.

THE NIGERIAN TELCO WAR: ETISALAT'S BIG HAIRY AUDACIOUS GOAL

Global politics and diplomacy may not be able to totally avoid wars, but the global community has found a way to still ensure a semblance of fairness even in the prosecution of war with the guidance of the Geneva Convention. That is why War Generals can still be prosecuted for war crimes at the international court of justice. Attacks against children, women and civilian populations are taken seriously. Crimes of rape and genocide are condemned. Use of children as soldiers receive international disapproval. The world is saying all is not fair in war after all.

As good as this convention is, the marketing industry does not wholly subscribe to it. In marketing warfare, brands play hard and push the frontiers of their strategy to the limit. While there is a general subscription to equity, fairness and mutual respect in the prosecution of wars, challenger brands may sometimes break the rule to grab shares in a very competitive market and take on incumbents. Armed with this philosophy, challenger brands have taken on mega brands successfully, and in some other instances, at great costs.

ETISALAT VERSUS MTN

Etisalat is a challenger brand and the fourth entrant into the Nigerian GSM market. The brand came in with an irreverent atti-

69

tude reminiscent of the entrance of MTN into the same industry years earlier. Youthful, trendy and with a refreshing approach, the brand began to warm its way into the heart of Nigerians, especially the youth market that loves the gospel of 'freemium' promoted by the brand. Consumers love freebies. The youth market especially, is crazy about the magic word 'FREE'. The brand offered free data, free voice calls, free SMS and very competitive tariffs to strengthen its youthful profile. It soon became the fastest growing brand from its small base and was getting the highest share of new connections.

The brand hired a number of experienced hands from incumbent players in the industry, thus had good knowledge of how the incumbents thought and the strategy that drives each competitor. Bold and daring, the brand benchmarked itself against the market leader, and not the other incumbents: Globacom and Airtel. Insights from some staff members say the aim of the company is to be number two in the market from their number four position. This big, hairy and audacious goal makes the brand come after the market leader in very bold and sometimes brazen manners.

This laudable goal and inspiring ambition for a young brand galvanizes action and inspire staff to dare the impossible, think the unthinkable, and tread the grounds other brands would fear to tread. This ambition was given expression in strategy and execution excellence by Etisalat. Apart from the vantage position of learning from whatever best practices the incumbents had experienced, the brand also had the privilege of learning from the mistakes the incumbents made in its network infrastructure roll out, retail outlets strategy formulation and implementation, and customer engagement strategies.

In war strategy, a direct attack against an enemy's defence is hardly advocated. It wearies the attacker and heightens the resistance. An indirect approach is advocated, because it has the capacity to upset the balance of the opposition and weaken its hold. Challenger brands, however, break existing rules and make theirs to suit their ambitions. Etisalat ignored this maxim and boldly chose to directly challenge the MTN brand in some of its initiatives. These initiatives were bold statements about the brand's ambitions.

What looked like the first daring move by Etisalat was when some MTN high value customers began to receive SMS messages from Etisalat with offers of numbers similar to their MTN numbers but with the Etisalat code. Even senior management staff of MTN got such messages on their private MTN lines. The brand may have profiled all incoming numbers from other networks onto her network and isolated the heavy callers or engaged in a random selection of numbers and it was just accidental that the customers were high value customers. Better still, the high value customer database may have been legitimately bought from an organization that sells lists. What was of interest at this time was the boldness of the brand's action at openly prospecting customers from a market leader before Mobile Number Portability that allowed such acts became official.

The objective behind this strategy was clear. The brand wanted to be the preferred alternative line for high value customers on incumbent networks, while it focuses on recruiting new users amongst the huge youthful Nigerian population with love for freebies. This is ultimately designed to guarantee both market volume and value share in the long run. It is on record that the brand drove the growth of the multi-sim culture in Nigeria. This in turn drove wallet share that affected the incumbents negatively.

Not long after this, the brand ran an advertising campaign where one of MTN's propositions was satirized. The MTN proposition was called MTN Family and Friends, which offered a special low call rate to customers when they call their registered family and friends. Etisalat ran an advertising campaign for her own proposition offering bonus airtime to all networks and said in the advertising that it didn't matter who the customer was calling, friends, family or even enemies, the bonus could be used as the customer desired. Intelligent followers of the conversation in the advertising didn't need to do much to understand the references being made.

MTN engaged a popular movie star in Nigeria for two different advertising campaigns. Etisalat a few weeks later released an advertising campaign showing another notable actor in Nigeria offering exciting deals to Etisalat customers. In this advertising, a queue of willing prospects was formed and a guy dressed exactly like the movie star MTN had earlier used was seen on the queue with his yellow baseball cap. Yellow is MTN's brand color. This actor then went to the Etisalat model to avail himself of the offer. The Etisalat model showed surprise and was about to speak when the purported MTN model closed his mouth. The message was clear and succinct. Etisalat was saying in the advertising that the MTN star model found the Etisalat offer irresistible and made a switch. At a period when Mobile Number Portability (a regime that allows customers to switch between mobile network operators) hadn't formally started, this was a very bold statement.

These bold steps endeared the brand to the youths who saw the brand as a refreshing departure from the incumbents that were perceived as very matured and less trendy. The communication expression of the brand's strategy was also very youthful, daring and engaging. This profile was so strong such that even older customers who were still young at heart began to warm up to the brand. All these coupled with the 'Freemium' strategy drove market share increase at a very fast pace. The brand became the fastest growing brand in the Nigerian telecom history in the first five years of its existence. While it may not have come close to beating the market leader, the brand demonstrated an ambition that made the second and third place incumbents very uncomfortable, and gained the attention of the market.

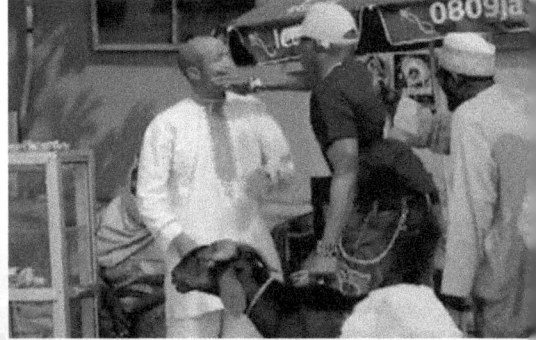

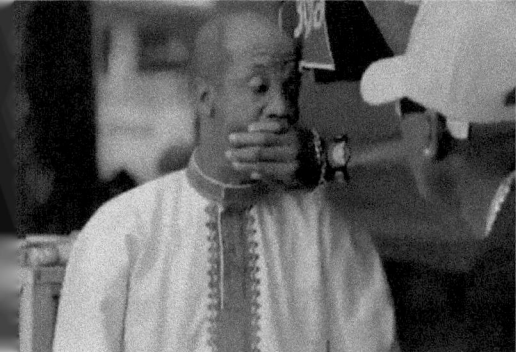

Screen dump of the Etisalat advertising

Screen Dumps of MTN advertising that may have been satirized

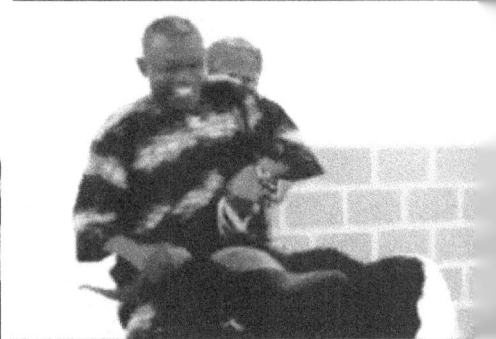

Screen Dumps of MTN advertising that may have been satirized

CHAPTER NINE

FIRST TO MARKET VERSUS BEST TO MARKET

I was raised in a marketing school where First To Market was a holy grail. You must do everything humanly and strategically possible to ensure you beat competition to the market. This is almost paranoia amongst marketers. Sometimes, the maxim is 'Don't wait for perfection, Correct as you go'. This holds true to a large extent. However, it is not absolute and care needs to be taken to ensure that haste does not become waste, especially in the area of technology where new breakthroughs and advancement push an early morning's innovation into obsolescence in the early evening.

TELECOM OPERATORS' LAUNCH OF BLACKBERRY INTO NIGERIA: GLOBACOM VERSUS MTN

Glo was the first telecom operator to launch Blackberry into the Nigerian market. The brand made a big deal out of it. It was positioned for the very high value customers, who were on post-paid packages. The communication message and cues were very aspirational. It was meant for royalty. Even the layout of the advertising material was in royal colors, royal purple. While the brand enjoyed the first to market posture, it was launched into a market that is predominantly prepaid. Most of the very high value customers in Nigeria then were on prepaid. Though they qualified as royalty by virtue of their income and social status, the Blackberry from Glo was beyond their reach.

MTN was a late entrant into the Blackberry adoption and usage marketing space. When the brand decided to get into the space, the brand chose to demystify and democratize the device. MTN negotiated and got the opportunity of introducing the first prepaid Blackberry in Africa. In a market that is about 98% prepaid, it was an instant success. Sales grew phenomenally to the recognition of Blackberry, the manufacturer. The market hardly remembered that Glo was first to market. It was no longer relevant. What the industry remembered was the brand that was best to market in terms of relevance to consumer needs.

Speed to market is important. First to market is still a very critical success factor in marketing warfare. In spite of this, it is important not to sacrifice quality and relevance for speed. This is not just important for new launches. It is also important for competitive responses. When you hit the panic button because a competitor has launched a major initiative and you give a knee-jerk response, you may either respond rashly and foolishly in haste without a thorough analysis, or you may copy blindly only to discover you have made a huge error. A brand once copied a competitor's initiative so hurriedly that it made the

> If you are in a category where the cost of switching is low, then it is critical not just to be the first, but also to be the best.

exact mistakes the competitor made even in the advertising! It was a classic case of how not to copy or react hurriedly.

Best to Market strategy chooses to respond to competitor's initiative or innovation with an improved version of the launched product or service in record time. This is done so well and launched so spectacularly that the first organization to launch loses the first mover advantage, attention, recall and relevance. Strategy and contextual balance is the rule here. By all means possible, try to be the first and the best in the market! If you are in a category where the cost of switching is high, first to market is the rule, but be nimble with upgrades where necessary so you can continue to remain competitive. If you are in a category where the cost of switching is low, then it is critical not just to be the first, but also to be the best.

CHAPTER TEN

CONTINUOUS PROMOTION: STRICTLY THE SIGN OF A SICK BRAND?

In my days as a marketing management practitioner in a manufacturing and marketing FMCG Company, the maxim that 'continuous promotion is the sign of a sick brand' held sway. Continuous promotion was seen as an indicator that all is not well with the brand in question. It meant that the core product or proposition was not compelling and relevant enough to command patronage on its own except there is an inducement. This elevates a tactical tool to the level of the strategic. Consumer promotions are short term initiatives meant to achieve short term objectives, which help the delivery of the long term or strategic goals. Conversely, when it is done back to back by a brand, it speaks to trouble.

Once upon a time in Nigeria, a brand of carbonated drink was known for back-to-back consumer promotions, sometimes running through the year. The Brand's credibility began to suffer after a while, and when the consumer promotions stopped, the brand almost died. It suffered a significant setback that has taken years to recover from. Even though the carbonated drink market went through a tough time, other brands continued to grow. New brands came on the scene and have since gained substantial market share. This brand is still struggling to restate itself back to the prominence and market share it used to command.

While this assertion is true in the FMCG sector, any marketer desirous of success in a different sector should re-examine the maxim for relevance and applicability; otherwise, such brands will pay dearly. Such a sector is the mobile telecommunication sector. Differentiation in core product here is near impossible, because the core product is generic. Quality of service, distribution, Go-to-market strategies and brand power can offer some level of differentiation, but many of them are not sustainable, because competitors can achieve parity on most fronts. The base products are therefore often taken for granted. That is why the brand and its emotional connection with the target customers is very critical.

Deals, discounts, freebies, etc., are the norm in this category. Consumers here are smart enough to understand that apart from the brand, the services are not so differentiated. Thus, the category records a high incidence of multi-sim ownership. The intention is two-fold: multi-sim allows the consumer bargain-hunt and get the best of all the discounts and freebies available in the market; it also allows the customer to have an alternative network to make his calls in the event that any of the networks had any technical challenge.

Therefore, it is suicidal if your competitor in the telecommunication space is running a promotion and you ignore it. It can cost you dearly. This is because the reaction of a significant segment of the market is near instant to promotions. Immediate migration of spend is observed as consumers go after the deals and the freebies. They take their minutes away from you to the network offering the deals, and either come back when the deal is over, or when you raise a counter offer, or match what the competitor offered. A day is enough to notice such migrations. It hits your revenue immediately. You can see the shortfall in your minutes of use and revenue instantly. Hence, you are left with very little choices but to react to whatever deals go on in the market. Not responding can be costly. The customers will see you as stingy and tilt the share of wallet scale against your brand. It is very difficult to ignore this reality, so you may find yourself running back-to-back consumer promotions. At this point, it is not your brand that is sick, it is the entire market.

STRONG WINDS AGAINST A BRAND'S SOUL: MTN AND THE TELECOM PRICE WAR

In 2012, the Nigerian mobile telecommunication space became very tough and extremely competitive. Price became a major tool for perceived competitive advantage. Price slashes, freebies and discounts became the order of the day. Consumers were offered deals to recharge their phone lines and get five times the value of their spend. The deals were so aggressive that sound business managers began to wonder how the companies were going to remain profitable. However, market share was the focus and the aggressiveness continued. Operators were practically buying market share with discounts and freebies. A new economy aptly described as the 'Freemium Economy' had evolved. MTN held back in the first quarter of that year and refused to join the fray. This made the propositions in the Brand's stable very uncompetitive when stacked up against the market. The brand became over two hundred percent more expensive than the market on some of her propositions. The brand got punished by the consumers who took their minutes elsewhere and MTN began to see some market share erosion. The market share loss came with it a corresponding increase in share of wallet, and so revenue suffered too. Customers were picking up the sim cards of other networks and sharing the revenue the brand used to own exclusively with other networks.

The brand soon realized that her puritan stand to save the industry from the horrors of a price war was not in her favour and changed her strategy. A price reduction of over 40% was effected and aggressive promotions kicked in. The brand took a conscious decision to match the most aggressive offer in the market. With this decision taken by the market leader, the market became more convoluted with offers and deals, as each operator tried to outdo the other. Consumers were daily accumulating free minutes that they were required to use up within specified time frames. Efforts to use the free minutes before expiration put tremendous pressure on the networks and quality suffered. This scenario worsened until the regulator stepped in with a ban on all promotions by all the operators to give room for quality of service improvements.

This ban was lifted in the second quarter of 2013 and the consumer promotion madness continued. Any brand manager with a fixed notion of continuous consumer promotions being the sign of a sick brand in such a category will soon go extinct. Continuous consumer promotions can indeed be the sign of sick brands, but this may not be universal to all categories and all markets. This rule simply did not apply in the commoditized Nigerian telecom market, and possibly in similar categories with similar dynamics in other markets. An apt conclusion here could be that continuous promotion could be the sign of a sick industry.

CHAPTER ELEVEN

HEAD-ON AGAINST A PREVAILING CULTURE? MAYBE NOT

Culture is a very deep concept that defines who we are and significantly informs what we do. Cultures are often driven by belief systems that run deep beneath the surface of the human makeup. It is resident in the portion of the iceberg beneath the surface of the sea. Big and bold brands can attempt to change a prevailing culture, but it is usually a costly adventure. Smart brands and companies can however enhance a prevailing culture, promote it or build businesses around it.

The consumption culture for alcoholic beverages in Nigeria is not an in-home consumption culture. While a sizeable proportion is done in the home or during parties at home, breweries cannot sustain their businesses by the volume that gets consumed at such events. Rather, the bulk of the sales and consumption that sustain the breweries are done at the bars out of the home and amongst friends with specific ambient accompaniments. Common interests like soccer get shared during such moments over drinks. Personal victories like promotions get celebrated with friends at the bar and the 'boys' unwind at the club to catch up on the goings on. The bar is also where men 'drown their sorrows' in drinks. It will be pure suicide for any alcoholic beverage brand to attempt to change this culture.

CADBURY'S CHEF PEPPER SOUP CUBES; AHEAD OF ITS TIME OR HEAD-ON AGAINST AN INGRAINED CULTURE?

Pepper soup is a spicy Nigerian delicacy believed to be medicinal and a perfect companion to the consumption of alcohol. Most bars and clubs therefore ensure they have people with culinary expertise in the preparation of this delicacy. A mark of the originality and efficacy of this delicacy is in its spicy taste and a special kind of leaves and seeds believed to be the medicinal ingredients. Pepper soup also gets consumed in the home as part of normal meals, and sometimes on recommendation for new mothers. The in-home consumption is however very small in comparison to the consumption in bars.

In the mid 90s, Cadbury Nigeria developed a new product branded Chef Pepper Soup Cubes. The company processed the local ingredients for making pepper soup and pressed them into cubes. It was marketed on the convenience platform as a convenient way to enjoy the delicacy that Nigerians love. It was meant to take away the hassles women go through to prepare the delicacy and enhance in-home consumption.

The brand was launched with a lot of fanfare. The product tasted great. The packaging was beautiful. The advertising was excellent. Not long after this, Nestlé, a competitor also launched Maggi Pepper soup cubes. Despite the efforts and resources put behind the two brands, they both failed and have disappeared from the Nigerian brand landscape. I am sure there are analyses that both companies may have done to understand why both brands failed. I am however persuaded that a major factor responsible for the failure is that both brands tried to change a prevailing ingrained culture.

I was part of the marketing team behind Chef Pepper soup cubes and had firsthand consumer and trade feedback. We combed

83

Circumstances, situations, accidents and incidents can either conspire or individually shape culture within time contexts.

many 'pepper soup joints' during the launch to introduce the brand. The taste was great. Consumers liked it, but three problems reared their heads. Consumers couldn't see their beloved medicinal leaves in the pepper-soup made from Chef Pepper-soup cubes. Secondly, the bar owners were used to their own process of selecting, mixing and cooking the delicacy that they considered less expensive. The new nicely packaged and branded pepper soup cubes were considered more expensive and disempowered them as it limited their influence on the taste. The fear of losing their customers who wanted to see their herbal leaves in their pepper-soup made continuity of usage a challenge. With low patronage from this critical group and the inability of in-home consumption to sustain the business, it didn't take long before the product failed.

This example is not an exhaustive study of Chef Pepper-soup cubes and Maggi Pepper-soup cubes. There may be other reasons that may have been behind the failures, but I believe the attempt at changing a prevailing culture was core to the trouble the brands had, in addition to possible cost issues. It may be safer for companies to understand the underlying culture, values, beliefs and deep-rooted emotions behind consumer actions per time, and build their brands around its enhancement, enjoyment and promotion, instead of pitching the brands against it.

This assertion is however not absolute. Culture evolves and consumers change. Circumstances, situations, accidents and incidents can either conspire or individually shape culture within time contexts. Sometimes, some brands may be ahead of their times, because they were birthed way ahead of consumer readiness for same. This was the case with Poundo Yam; a product conceived, produced and marketed by Cadbury Nigeria Plc, now Kraft Foods, back in the 80s.

POUNDO YAM: LIGHT YEARS AHEAD OF ITS TIME

Pounded Yam is considered as the most popular and most respected kind of meal in the South West, South East and the Middle belt regions of Nigeria. Made from boiled yam, it is pounded until it becomes a smooth thick paste, hard enough to be eaten with washed hands or cutlery, soft enough to be swallowed with various soup types. To many traditional connoisseurs of the meal, the pounding process is almost a ritual, and is even believed to add to the special taste of the meal. It is however a laborious process that requires strength and special skills for a perfect finish.

Cadbury saw potentials in the popularity of this meal and decided to exploit it by developing convenience into the process to eliminate labour and time. The company developed Poundo Yam by pre-processing Yam, which is the primary product, into Yam Powder that could be mixed in boiled water and stirred into pounded yam, thus eliminating the pounding process and making the delicacy easily available to connoisseurs. As it turned out, the product failed. Even when it was focused on the export market, it still failed to survive. Nigerians wanted their yam pounded the traditional way, because they did not believe the pre-processed and stirred yam tasted the same with traditional pounded yam. The company had to discontinue Poundo Yam.

However, as time went by, the social economic environment went through fundamental changes. More women emerged in the corporate world, and with the emergence came sophistication and the need to juggle career and family life within the limit of a 24-hour day. Convenience and increased outdoor lifestyle became major factors in shaping culture. A lot of women no longer had the time to cook and pound yam as it was in times past. It was also out of sync with the sophisticated lifestyle and modernity the new women had embraced. Physical pounding of yam by the 21st century woman was no longer considered appropriate for her status. An alternative was required. Increasing time spent out of the home by both husbands and wives also developed the fast food culture, and soon the fast food chains grew. The average Nigerian, however, still wanted his African delicacy in a fast food environment, especially pounded yam. The fast food chains began to create new lines of products for African cuisine to exploit this need. Pounded Yam was top on the list; but the Eateries could not cope with demand if the traditional way of preparing pounded yam continued.

These two factors: convenience for the new career woman, and convenience and turnover for the managers of the fast food companies created an opportunity for the return of pre-processed yam that can be stirred in hot water to produce this delicacy in a quicker fashion. Smart business folks cashed in on this opportunity and the same Poundo Yam concept that failed in the eighties into the early 90s has today become a success. It hugely enjoys both in-home and out of home consumption. It came ahead of its time in its first coming, but has re-emerged at the right time when the market was ready. A lot of companies are making good money producing and marketing various brands of this product now. Time tempers culture. This may also be the challenge of the pepper soup cubes brands. As the female executive gets increasingly busier and pepper soup possibly becomes a more staple delicacy in the home, the busy female executive juggling the home and career may occasion a re-emergence of the product in a different form. Some variant are already emerging in pockets of outlets.

CHAPTER TWELVE

GOING FOR BROKE: CONCENTRATE YOUR FORCES FOR THE KILL!

In war, concentration of force is a strategy that demands synchronization and deployment of superior firepower to realize specific objectives or win specific battles that can define or redefine the war. In such instances, nothing is left to chance. A full deployment of resources is employed in concert to ensure a decisive outcome. This same principle is critical for success in marketing warfare. There are some must-win battles that require a concentration of force. These battles can either change the course of the war or determine ultimate victory.

There are volume and/or value market share battles that must be fought with everything an organization or a marketer has got. Sometimes, it is winning new businesses that can alter the organization's fortunes significantly. At other times, it is gaining the confidence of regulatory authorities, or seeking for empathy from government to effect favorable policies that will enhance operations and profitability. Once you define the status of the battle and it qualifies for a concentration of force principle, you don't leave any stone unturned. Failure is not an option in such a battle. Winning becomes a paranoia.

WINNING THE MTN ACCOUNT: THE DDB CASERS STORY

Winning or losing accounts in the advertising business comes with heightened emotions that could be positive or negative, depending on how the outcome affects each organization and individuals involved. It is usually a market share war that sometimes translates either into a financial boom or colossal losses. When large accounts are won or lost, it can spell the demise of a loser and herald the transformation of small or medium sized organizations into market leaders. When large accounts are up for pitches therefore, competing organizations make significant investments in sourcing data, hiring resources, and buying up the latest technological assets that they believe can help make the right impressions and sway decisions their way. Payment of pitch fees has been advocated in the marketing and advertising industries to ensure organizations that do not succeed at securing whatever business they pitched for can have a soft landing and at least recoup their investment. Such fees may however not be able to cover certain costs that may have been incurred while trying to win blue chip accounts. One advertising agency in Nigeria that the payment of any pitch fee would have amounted to nothing to if the organization had lost the pitch for the MTN account is DDB Lagos. The amount invested in the pitch remains a landmark in the annals of the history of advertising pitches in Nigeria.

DDB Lagos started out as Casers, an agency with an attitude. The agency positioned itself to appeal to only a select clientele that could afford its expensive, but robust marketing and advertising creative services. Strategy was core to the agency. Sound marketing thinking was its edge. It was driven by a desire to be both a marketing partner to its clients and an advertising creative service agency, based on the view of the founder, who was a marketing management professional, that the quality of input into the advertising process could be better than it was. Unlike other agencies that were located on the less expensive Lagos mainland in Nigeria,

DDB Lagos chose to open shop in high brow Ikoyi area of Lagos Island. By this singular factor, it defined its kind of clients. They were few, but wealthy. The agency too was small, but rich. The owners however realized that the strategy was not sustainable if the agency wanted to play in the big league. Scale was critical as the accounts grew. It did become apparent that the agency needed to change direction. This it did and moved to the mainland.

Large accounts were attracted, and the agency grew into a medium size organization; became an affiliate of DDB Worldwide; changed its name from Casers to DDB Casers, then later DDB Lagos, and got a good piece of a juicy telecommunication account. DDB Lagos resigned this telecommunication account after having been paid a fairly large sum of debt it was being owed at about the time MTN, the leading telecommunication company, put its advertising services business up for a pitch. When DDB Lagos got invited, the agency founder saw the invitation as a redefining moment for the organization and took a personal decision that the pitch was a critical battle that had to be won. He saw it as a victory that could change the fortunes of the business forever and concluded that a concentration of force was required to win.

He took the first decision to prepare a financial war chest. He instructed the company accountant to ensure the money paid by the telecommunication account the agency had resigned was not spent on anything. It was reserved for the war! He then contacted the DDB global network and asked for the Group's best strategy resource in telecommunication advertising. While the Group sought for the person that fitted his requirement, he assembled his local team made up of strategists, creative people and two marketing consultants; one of which was a celebrated marketing director of a multinational company, who had just retired, and another who also had a reputation as an excellent marketing management professional.

The DDB network finally found him a strategist in telecommunication marketing communication, but she could not get a visa to come to Nigeria. When all efforts to get her a visa failed, the founder made up his mind not to spare anything to win the account. He took the decision to get her to fly to South Africa and also flew the locally assembled team of ten to South Africa to work on the brief. This team spent a week in South Africa at great expense, even though not much came from the international resource. The local team eventually came back to Nigeria to conclude work on the pitch. At the presentation, technology failed the agency when it came to the creative side of the pitch, and a convincing leap could not be made from strategy to creativity. Nevertheless, the strategy was so strong, it got acknowledgement from the pitch panel. Hence, the agency made it to the second round of the pitch based on the strength of her strategic thinking.

In preparation for the second round, the agency founder made up his mind to give the pitch all he had. He made contacts across the advertising industry within and beyond Africa for the best creative mind that can work on the brief with his agency. Having been scored very highly in strategy, he was ready to ensure the required leap from strategy to creativity was made. He eventually was pointed in the direction of Graham Warsop, a British writer and founder of one of the most awarded agency in South Africa then, The Jupiter Drawing Room. At a significant cost to the founder of DDB Casers, Graham Warsop agreed to work on the creative side of the presentation. He later turned in excellent creative works that the agency found mind blowing.

Then again, the challenge was how the Nigerian team will present the excellent creative work done by Graham if he was not on ground to make the presentation himself. To accomplish this task, a psychologist was hired, and for days, all the members of the team were holed up in a hotel, where the MTN conference room for the pitch presentation would take place. The psychologist worked with each presenter on how to make each presentation great. This was also at a significant cost. Every element of the presentation was rigorously rehearsed until the team was sure they would deliver the excellent creative work as well as Graham and possibly better than Graham. All these investments and con-centration of forces paid off. The agency won the account and its fortune changed. According to the founder, he would have offered himself to be fired if the agency had lost the pitch because of the level of financial risk he took.

This is a classic case of throwing everything you have into a war, shutting the door to the possibility of failure and going for broke. If the agency had lost the pitch, the loss would have been signifi-cant. While this action could not have guaranteed absolute suc-cess, as other things could have gone wrong, it however greatly increased the probability of success. If the prize is considered transformational to the organization, concentration of forces for victory is a wise choice.

CHAPTER THIRTEEN

TRANSLATING STRATEGY TO ACTION

War Generals know that the best of strategies are only as good as the execution. The men on the field determine the success or failure of strategy by their action or inaction in the faithful and timely execution of strategy. It is the same in Marketing. The best marketing strategy is useless without excellent execution. The truth really is that your execution is your strategy. It doesn't matter how fanciful your PowerPoint presentation is or how excellent your marketing plan looks, what is most important; what impacts the consumer; what creates the desired action is execution. Faithful and excellent execution of strategy is what the customer experiences. It is the true expression of your strategy. It is therefore what gets measured. It is the determinant of success or failure. If it is shoddy, your strategy is shoddy. Forget the fact that you got an award at the annual marketing and brand strategy conference. What is most critical is how you translate the strategy into action. Your PowerPoint is your intention. The customer doesn't care about that intention. The customer is only interested in what you do.

Translating strategy into action therefore requires as much rigor as is required in crafting the strategy. Inadequate planning automatically yields poor output or execution. Some brands are so cash loaded that they throw money at everything. The size of your budget is not necessarily a success factor here. Sometimes, a small budget can be a blessing. It forces you to think deeply on how to maximize value from your limited resources. Too much money can cause mental laziness that occasion wastage. This is not an advocacy for low budgets. Effective budgeting is the key. Poor funding of great ideas can turn a brand into an ideas incubator for better-funded brands.

Therefore, execution planning is a discipline on its own. Thorough planning, correct identification of priorities, efficient resource allocation, effective deployment, management and monitoring are required to ensure a faithful delivery of strategy in action.

PLAN WITH THE ELEMENTS

Strategy execution in marketing does not happen inside cosy offices, but in the rough and sometimes, dirty market place. Such markets in parts of Africa are not structured, clean and covered. They are open-air markets where trillions exchange hands daily in environments that the dignified or sophisticated white-collar person may not find comfortable. In parts of Africa, marketers who do not understand the dynamics of these markets and devise effective ways to engage them may struggle to succeed.

Sometimes, in the heat of project delivery and speed to market pressures, marketers often forget to plan with the elements in mind,

It doesn't matter how fanciful your PowerPoint presentation is, or how excellent your marketing plan looks, what is most important; what impacts the consumer; what creates the desired action is execution.

93

despite the fact that they have to execute in the open market. Nature has a way of playing games on mortal man, especially when we take her for granted. Excellent execution of strategy has often been marred by nature when it is taken for granted. We have had comical situations in Nigeria where people who are reputed to have supernatural powers have been engaged to prevent rain from disrupting major outdoor brand events.

This is a live challenge in a country like Nigeria where there is a dearth of large indoor venues for Events and Activations. Brands and marketers are compelled to hold events outdoor with the attendant risk of rainfall. Marquees get erected, but can mean nothing when a windy rainstorm strikes. The alternative is to avoid any major brand event during the rainy season. This is very difficult to pull through. It can force the brand into seasonality.

Once upon a time, a big launch by a major brand was marred by the elements. An element of the launch was meant to have a helicopter drop content-loaded balloons across the city. A royal horse parade was meant to complement this on the ground. Unfortunately, even though the plan was around a period when rain was meant to pause for a while, the August break, a stormy rain chose that day to unleash its terror. Not only were the horsemen drenched and their beautiful and colorful robes messed up, the stormy wind blew the balloons beyond the scope intended and the people who were meant to catch the secret gifts couldn't get the balloons. It was a disaster! This was a great idea marred by nature.

The safest way to avoid such a mishap is not to plan such an event for the rainy season, though the winds itself can do much harm without the rain. This means big events that cannot be activated indoors would either require spiritual interventions to avoid disruptions or must be avoided during certain seasons. Plan around the elements as a good war strategist. Avoidance of a clash with nature is wise, but you can also exploit nature by integrating the elements into your key success factors.

CHAPTER FOURTEEN

STUDY YOUR BATTLEFIELD WELL

A critical element in warfare is an understanding of the battle terrain. Success in war requires a good understanding of the battlefield, because every battle terrain has its peculiarities that if well understood could be used to advantage by an astute war general or strategist. Military intelligence, amongst other things, study battle terrains to devise optimal strategies that can leverage on the environment to aid victory. Insufficient information on the battlefield can lead to fatalities in battles. The best armed army and the most disciplined of soldiers can be decimated due to insufficient understanding of the battlefield.

Just as this is a reality in war, it is also a reality in marketing. A good understanding of the political, economic, social, cultural and technological competitive terrain is critical to avoid fatalities. Your good intentions are immaterial and cannot excuse your ignorance about the market and its dynamics. Some brands have made bold entries into new markets without a full understanding of the socio-political, economic, cultural, regulatory and technological realities of the new markets. They went into the new markets with templates of what worked in a different market and expected direct application and adoption. The market has punished many of such brands.

Kenya is the biggest East African economy with its own peculiarities. Kenyan consumers are patriotic brand loyalists, who buy proudly Kenyan goods without apologies. Kenyan entrepreneurs are also significantly more sophisticated and more competitive with developed systems, procedures and processes than a lot of other African markets. In addition to this, they are deeply patriotic. The regulatory environment in Kenya is also peculiar and requires very good understanding for any brand that wants to operate successfully in Kenya.

Post apartheid, South African based companies began investing in other African markets and soon became the third largest investor in some of the African countries after the United Kingdom and United States of America. Their operational mode was however to set up shop to compete with incumbents in the countries, and because of their access to capital, they focused on outspending incumbents in such nations in technology, modern equipment and manufacturing processes and marketing. Management teams of some of these companies were also top heavy with expatriates that were very sound professionals, but who sometimes exhibited domineering mindsets and did not connect with key stakeholders within the government and regulatory environments. This strategy failed woefully in Kenya.

SABMILLER'S FIRST ENTRY AND THE HURRIED EXIT FROM KENYA

The peculiarities of the Kenyan market made it impossible for big brands like SABMiller with all its global reputation to have a foothold in the Kenyan market in its first attempt. The brand did not fully understand and respond with appropriate strategies to what the Kenyan market required and had to beat an expensive retreat. SABMiller established its own brewery in Kenya with Castle larger beer as its flagship brand. However, it was in for a shocker, as Kenya's East African Breweries Limited, east and central Africa's largest brewer, gave SABMiller a hard run for its money.

East African Breweries Limited used her Tusker brand, marketed on the 'my country my beer' platform to combat SABMiller's Castle Larger. This was a powerful platform in a country with citizens that exude nationalistic pride and fierce loyalty to home grown brands. The two brands engaged in a bitter battle that eventually saw SABMiller close shop under a year of its entry into the market. The company eventually sold its manufacturing plant to East African Breweries Limited. Tusker beer till date remains the highest selling brand of beer in the East and central African market. SABMiller did not return to Kenya until almost ten years later, via the acquisition of Crown Foods. Other South African brands that had similar experiences in the Kenyan market were Numetro and Media24, South Africa's largest publishing company.

Some other South African brands like Tiger Brands, and the financial and media entertainment services brands like Multichoice, Woolworth and Stanbic Bank, however, found a way around the Kenyan peculiarities and are doing very good business in Kenya. Tiger Brands is South Africa's largest fast-moving consumer goods company. The company bought a controlling stake in Haco Industries Kenya, and has grown the business significantly since its Kenyan market entry. The joint venture partnership fostered a winning combination of manufacturing and technical expertise from Tiger brands with the local operating knowledge and consumer connection guidance from Kenyan Haco management and directors.

It sounds incredible that a global brand like SABMiller would find it impossible to penetrate and exploit the huge opportunities in the Kenyan market, but it is true. It is a testimonial to the truth that if brands do not mind the gap in local knowledge and understand the market they prospect, it can be disastrous. A good understanding of the battle terrain is critical to defining effective strategies that facilitate success. Tiger Brands understood this and used it to her advantage. SABMiller did not and paid dearly for it. The company however took its learning. SABMiller's re-entry into Kenya and its entry into Nigeria recognized the lessons of the initial Kenyan experience and mirrored Tiger Brands' entry strategy.

CHAPTER FIFTEEN

ALL IS FAIR IN WAR? WHO PAID FOR THIS MERCHANDISING?

The Tanzanian government at some point in the nation's history nationalized all companies and the state took ownership and control. Though, after a while, it was discovered that the government was not structured to run the corporations efficiently. A decision was taken to sell the corporations back to the private sector investors. A lot of companies bought back the control of their brands and assets in Tanzania, but British American Tobacco lost the bid to take back her brands and assets in Tanzania to a competing company, Aspen. Thus, Aspen owned British American Tobacco brands in Tanzania. This was not a very exciting scenario for British American Tobacco that operates a thriving enterprise in Kenya. When Aspen cigarette therefore showed up in Kenya, the reaction by BAT was furious and fast.

The company moved swiftly into the trade and aggressively engaged the channels. Managers and executives shunned the comfort of their air-conditioned offices for the sweaty streets and the shops. Stocks of the Aspen cigarette brand had some of the fastest sales successes in history. The cigarettes simply disappeared. Customers sold out in record time! It would appear as though the Aspen sales team were crack professionals, who could sell anything, including snow to Eskimos. Unconfirmed reports however, said the BAT team mopped up the stocks. Customers who had sampled the product just could not get a stick to buy and so conversion was impossible.

At this point, Aspen had not set up any manufacturing infrastructure in Kenya. The stock that was sold initially was imported into the country and so replenishment required further importation. This was at a point when the 'Proudly Kenyan' nationalistic emotions ran very high and imported brands were not favorites. Hence, a very lethal blow was dealt the Aspen brand when some merchandising materials appeared in the trade with the bold caption: 'Aspen. Imported'. It was a most effective way to de-market Aspen in the Kenyan market. No one knew who paid for and placed the merchandising materials, but the fate of the brand was sealed. It had to leave Kenya.

THIS AIN'T NO DUMP SITE MATE!
THE DETERGENT WAR: P&G'S ARIEL VERSUS UNILEVER'S OMO

Procter and Gamble is the big gorilla in the sanitary pad market in Kenya with close to 80% share. The company had a good understanding of the Kenyan market and was not expected to encounter any difficulty in moving and winning in new categories. Its first attempt at the detergent market however ended up in a hasty retreat.

Ariel was introduced into the Kenyan market, where Unilever's Omo was the big gorilla. Shortly afterwards, some damaging information began to circulate across the nation that Omo was corrosive and harsh on women's hands. This had a telling effect on the brand, and the brand had to react by embarking on consumer education to contain the damage. Washing Points were set up at every shopping mall and areas of high density to demonstrate how to use the brand. Women and washers were educated that they needed to soak their fabrics first with the detergent before the washing itself to prevent any reaction on the hands.

This strategy worked and the fear abated. The brand then went on to aggressively engage consumers on the effectiveness of the detergent at removing stubborn stains, while being gentle on the skin. Ariel responded with a BOGOF (Buy One Get One Free) consumer promotion, and Unilever went to court. At this point, Ariel was not manufactured in Kenya, it was imported. Unilever submitted that a BOGOF promo by an imported brand amounted to dumping. This was a powerful position to occupy at a point in the history of the nation when the 'Proudly Kenyan' sentiment was high, Ariel could not win the legal battle. The promo had to be stopped and the brand retreated. It has since re-entered the market, and is to date, a very strong number two. Unilever has had to go to court to challenge the brand's comparative communication that seems to denigrate a competitor, claiming the reference was to the Omo brand. The case was yet to be determined as at the time of this book's publication. It may turn out to be a classic in how challenger brands with clear focus and long-term vision can unseat a market leader.

CHAPTER SIXTEEN

BE BOLD OR BE BLOWN

Boldness, courage, and strength of character are fundamental qualities of successful soldiers. They also hallmark successful marketers. You must be daring enough to take bold steps that can change the competitive landscape. Bold and daring brands define or redefine the competitive terrain. Courage makes the difference between successful brands and brands destined to fail. There are times when a brand manager needs to take decisions that can be so fundamental that it can make or mar the fortunes of the brand for good.

REPOSITIONING CADBURY'S BOURNVITA: A DANGEROUS GAMBLE

Up until 1997, Cadbury's Bournvita was positioned as a vitality drink for the family. It was running neck to neck with Nestlé Milo for market volume leadership. However, Milo had a much more vibrant and premium perception amongst consumers, and so commanded more premium pricing.

Milo's bull eye target was children, and the brand was, and still is, positioned as the food drink of future champions. These tie into the end value aspiration of mothers, who desire their children to

101

win in life. The packaging exuded and still exudes youthfulness with real life models on the can. The marketing communication about the brand was vibrant. The mnemonics were exciting. The cues were aspirational. Children loved the brand.

On the other hand, Bournvita was targeted at the family, positioned on the platform of vitality. The packaging design was mature, the color was brown reflective of the beverage's cocoa base and the images on the can were silhouettes of active adult individuals. The brand was clearly not positioned for children, and so didn't reflect the vibrancy and youthfulness children love. Adults however, loved the brand and it commanded huge volume sales.

However, the market was changing rapidly around this time. Adult consumers were becoming more health conscious. Weight loss and healthy living were gaining currency. Unfortunately, cocoa beverage was perceived to make consumers fat. Hence, adult consumers were migrating to tea and coffee, and doing less of cocoa beverage. For a brand targeted at active adults, Bournvita began to suffer market share losses. This was in addition to consumer feedback of sediments and bitter after taste, dark looks attributed to low milk content by the consumers. There were even some unconfirmed and possibly malicious stories that it gave some consumers headaches.

Milo was perfectly positioned to exploit the Bournvita loss. As a brand targeted at children, it had no problem with migration issues. While Bournvita seemed to be focused on an expiring generation, Milo was focused of the emerging generation and future spenders with present pester power. The Milo brand kept growing. Bournvita on its own part needed a bold turn around, if it was to regain lost share.

Changing the fortune of the Bournvita brand required fundamental changes in product formulation, target customer definition, positioning, packaging and its communication. This was crucial and dangerous. As the company's flagship and cash cow, any error could be disastrous. Courage was required to take the bold leap in repositioning. The risk of dissonance with the huge loyal consumers was high, but the demand of change to avoid extinction was also real. The brand was in a place where it either took the bold leap to change or it stood the risk of being blown away by the hurricane of changing consumer tastes and preferences.

Various relevant researches conducted by the brand confirmed consumers' dissonance with the bitter after taste and sediment issue. The dark color was related to the dark packaging and perceived absence of milk. The reality of the changing consumer profile, taste and preference also came to the fore. The brand managers knew that change was inevitable. It was however a risk. The kind of huge volume being sold then was indicative of the fact that the brand still enjoyed huge patronage. Would the change irritate loyal consumers? Will they accept a new formulation? Will the new consumers the brand wanted to focus on accept the reformulated Bournvita? What if there is a rejection? What would happen not just to the brand, but the company herself? How will the trade take the change? How will the new formulation fare against Milo that had historically focused on children?

These questions were real and critical to the survival of the brand and the business, but something had to be done urgently. The company chose to bite the bullet and took the bold step. The product was reformulated and fortified with vitamins and minerals necessary for growing children. Based on research data confirmation that milky look and mouth-feel was important to children, the milk content was also enhanced. A bold move was made by the company to change the brand color from brown to royal purple. The packaging design was radically redesigned to be more contemporaneous in royal purple and yellow colors. For the first time, real life models were used on the packaging and the theme was focused on a mother and healthy looking children.

This repositioning was a bold and daring departure from the old. The new product was tastier, milkier and had a more rounded mouth-feel. Blind tests confirmed that the new product was not just better than the old, but also that children loved it, and it compared well with its competitor. Emboldened by this, the business took another daring step; the brand took a price increase! This was a most daring move to reverse the fortune of the brand and return it to profitability.

An excellent communication and launch plan focused heavily on children was developed and flawlessly executed. The focus of the communication was to tap into elements of the end value aspiration of mothers, anchored on cues that connect strongly with children. Some of the elements of mothers' aspirations the brand's new communication leveraged upon include the health and well-being of their children, mental alertness, excellence, and academic success. The repositioning campaign focused on the vitamins and minerals used to fortify the new product, related them to what they do in the body and connected them to the total wellbeing of the child.

The reformulated and repositioned brand was an instant success. Children loved it. Mothers embraced it. The trade supported it. The brand returned to profitability. Volume grew and the company became financially healthier. The risk paid off. The brand took

Packs of the old and the New Bournvita

the bold step it was most required to take and avoided the risk of being blown away. Not every brand can come back from the precipice of oblivion into market leadership. Bournvita did this at this point in the brand's life.

REDEFINING AN ANCILLARY INDUSTRY: MTN AND THE ADVERTISING INDUSTRY

If you are not a bold marketer, you can underperform your potentials and under-exploit the capacity of the brand. Bold brands redefine their category, break new grounds and are continual terrors to competition. Sometimes, bold brands can actually redefine a whole industry including ancillary industries. A good example of a bold brand's impact on an ancillary industry is MTN's impact on not just the telecommunication industry, but also the advertising industry.

When mobile telephony began in Nigeria, coverage and image were the two most powerful determinants of choice and adoption. In pursuit of brand gravitas in its image advertising drive, the MTN brand redefined the advertising industry in Nigeria with very disruptive creativity and daring executions. The brand led the revolution of full color printing by the print media. The best print media was until then only printing spot colours. The brand's preference for full process color press advertising changed the landscape and encouraged investments in full colour printing equipments by the media houses.

The first full music album launch by any brand was done by the MTN brand with the development, production and compilation of brand themed music in various genres on CDs. Radio stations in Nigeria for the first time gave airplay to good full-length brand music. It was a revolution. The TV commercials were not just great creative pieces, they were very powerful materials that gave the brand an emotional high ground. Consumers love them. They

105

spoke to the heart of the people and championed the dreams and aspirations of Nigerians for a new life full of exciting possibilities enabled by GSM.

The period between 2002 and 2005 was a golden age for disruptive advertising creativity and communication excellence. MTN, in partnership with her advertising agencies, TBWA and SO & U Advertising drove this change. Though a telecom brand, yet the brand fundamentally affected the Nigerian advertising landscape irrecoverably. It is a good example of how a brand's bold stance can transcend its boundaries to impact other categories. The Brand Managers built a humongous brand in the MTN brand at this time. Little wonder the brand not only became customers' first choice, but also grew phenomenally to become the indisputable market leader and attracted recognition by Interbrand. The brand till date remains boldly at the cutting edge of innovation and positively disruptive behaviour.

STILL TALKING BOLDNESS... PROVING PUNDITS WRONG: THE SO&U ADVERTISING STORY

An advertising agency brand emerged in the Nigerian marketing horizon in the early 80s with a very bold vision and a commitment to pursue and achieve its audacious dreams in spite of the daunting challenges of the times. Significant hurdles stood in the way of the promoters of the agency. The industry had a general belief that creative people could not run an advertising agency and if they did, they could not run it successfully. Most of the people running advertising agencies then were of Client Service backgrounds. A bunch of creative people out to run an advertising agency ran against the grain of the times. These were however a different breed of creative people. They were bold, audacious and driven by the passion to make a difference.

To worsen the scenario, the three promoters had no money and a very limited network of clients to start out. In spite of this, the team purposed to do things differently against all odds. They crafted a vision that they would do great advertising, targeting two distinct audiences: prospects and new entrants into advertising. They set themselves the target to be the most creative agency within twenty-four months, or at least one of the most creative in the industry within the same time frame. They also set themselves the target to be the agency that any student desirous of picking up advertising as a career would think of first as a place to build a career. They had the firm belief that great advertising was only possible with great people.

None of the three promoters had ever been a core marketing person in their careers until this point, so they had a deficit in marketing knowledge. They acknowledged this upfront and scheduled a 13-week in-house marketing crash course for all their staff across all functions, facilitated by a respected marketing professional. This immediately set them apart. Most agencies at the time only sent teams in the Client service and business development on marketing training, but here was an agency that even the creative people had marketing training. The difference soon began to show, as the agency began to win pitches against older and more known brands within two years of her life.

Creative people in agencies were usually kept at the back office and not client-facing. These folks therefore had very little network of their own to prospect for business. The team also acknowledged this and the team leader began a systematic process of networking himself into areas of influence in the advertising industry, the marketing industry, and the larger economy. He soon took on roles that gave him and his agency visibility and respect; assets he could leverage on to prospect business. His growing network combined with the passion to continuously do great works soon earned the agency the recognition, respect and kind of clientele the promoters wanted.

The products of these commitments were powerfully creative and refreshing within the Nigerian advertising industry then. Prospective clients walked into the agency on their own, based on the strength of the depth of marketing knowledge the agency consistently exhibited, as well as the excellent creativity, result oriented and award winning campaigns. All through the growing years, there were still convictions in different quarters that the agency was going to fail, because such an experiment had never been done before then.

These convictions fuelled a pathological fear of failure in the promoters, but they turned it into a positive propeller for success. It has been several years since this vision was crafted. The promoters have passionately committed themselves to it over the years, and today, it is one of the leading agencies in Nigeria with the Saatchi & Saatchi global affiliation and an impressive list of global brands on her clientele. This advertising agency is SO&U Saatchi. The promoters boldly dared to do the impossible when the industry did not give them a chance of success. The boldness paid off. The agency actually achieved her objective of being one of the most creative agencies in Nigeria within the first 18 months of her life. It remains a success story to date.

CHAPTER SEVENTEEN

THINK BIG, TALK BIG, ACT BIGGER

In war, rhetorics are as powerful as physical movement of troops into combat. Bold thinking, and sometimes, brash talking has the power to destabilize the opposition. Closely associated with boldness is the capacity to dream big, think big and act bigger. In product or service brand marketing, humility is not such a big virtue! Daring brands think big. They are not furtive. They take bold decisions and dare to thread where cowardly brands fear to go. If you want timeless resonance, then you must be ready to do what other brands are scared to do, say what other brands may be afraid to say; go where other brands are scared to go, so you can achieve what other brands may never be able to achieve.

There is a tendency to think only big brands can think big and act big. This is wrong thinking. Thinking big, talking big and acting even bigger is not only for big brands. Rather, it can be indicative of a clear vision and ambition by the manager of a very small or even new brand. Prima Garnet is a brand in the Nigerian advertising industry. When the brand launched into the market, it came into a market ruled by some powerful and established brands with foreign affiliates and big accounts. For a young, new and unknown brand to break clutter, get seen, get heard and get a good piece of the profitable business cake, it needed to do something shocking to the industry.

> **In product or service brand marketing, humility is not such a big virtue! Daring brands think big. They are not furtive. They take bold decisions and dare to thread where cowardly brands fear to go.**

Self-advertising was not common in the advertising industry then. When it got done, it was usually in specialized industry journals and hardly in the consumer newspapers. Prima Garnet changed the rule. The young unknown company went to town with a double page spread advertising smartly crafted to excite readers, intrigue the market and trigger curiosity in prospects.

The copy headline read 'We'll take your briefs to town' and showed different types of underwear on a cloth line. The brand was so bold and daring that it ran the advertising on a Sunday without the fear of what some puritans may say. It punned the word 'Brief' and sent a strong message to the industry about the Brand's boldness and capacity to challenge the status quo,

We'll take your briefs to town

The copy headline reading 'We'll take your briefs to town'

think and act beyond the norm.
Though the brand was young and unknown, it dreamt big and acted bigger. Brands willing to break clutter saw a partner in Prima Garnet, and despite being

young and unknown, the company attracted clients that found in Prima Garnet's brand philosophy, a sync with their own brand ethos and ambition. By the following Monday morning after the Sunday advertising ran in the newspaper, the agency's first big client went knocking on her door with a brief. Prima Garnet took this client's brand to great heights. It was the first brand to have its advertising exposed on CNN by any Nigerian advertising agency. Prima Garnet not only broke clutter, but has remained a leading and successful advertising agency brand to date.

PUSHING THE LIMITS:
THE KNORR CUBES STORY

Military invasions for territorial expansion and bold brand management require a continuous push against the limits and challenging established boundaries. It takes courage to do, but great dividends are impossible without daring disruptive behavior. Cadbury Nigeria was a Cadbury Schweppes company with Nigerians as majority shareholders. The company manufactured and marketed Cadbury brands locally, imported some and had franchises for brands from other companies. One of such brands was a seasoning brand, Knorr. The company competed in three broad categories: Food drinks, Confectionery and Food. The Knorr brand was the flagship of the Foods category. As at the mid to late 90s, the Knorr brand of seasoning was the highest value brand and the third largest in volume within the Cadbury portfolio of brands. Whenever it looked as if value target was going to be compromised, it was smarter for the business to sell additional cartons of Knorr than to sell equivalent volumes of the other brands with lower margins. The brand was therefore a very important brand within the portfolio. I took over the management of this brand in 1999.

However, the brand was number two in its category in volume. Maggi was the generic reference brand and number one in the seasoning category. It used to be a pain during market visits when the trade referred to Knorr with a prefix, Maggi Knorr. As far as the retail trade was concerned, all seasoning brands were Maggi. Knorr just happened to be a variant with a different colour and a different price point, even though quality perception was in favour of the Knorr brand. It was the Rolls Royce of the category. This strengthened our ability to price it at a premium.

In 2001, we decided to aggressively push the limit of the brand's performance and volume growth. We upped the ante in raising the brand's perception even higher with the conception of a new brand promise, new packaging design and payoff line graphically demonstrated in exciting advertising. We then conceived and executed a consumer promotion that had never been done by any brand in the category before. Historically, seasoning brands built their consumer promotions around the cube wrapper. Consumers therefore needed to send in specified numbers of these wrappers to qualify for prizes. This worked and considerable volume growths happened on each occasion.

However, we dared to do the impossible and changed this in 2001 with the bold move to request for trans-wraps or bags as entry requirements for a consumer promotion. We surmised that if we could pull this off, it was going to have a huge impact on trade uptake; that way we can achieve both push and pull to deliver the numbers. This sounded crazy! Skeptics thought we were making a grave mistake. Did we expect people to buy and throw away the cubes so they could qualify for the prizes? Did we expect people to consume more Knorr when it was not required? Where do we want them to keep the product after emptying the bag of 50 cubes? A few people thought it was a stupid idea, but we chose to attempt it. We also saw an opportunity to take a price increase based on the expected trade push. This was a margin booster for the brand and enhanced profitability. The consumer promotion was a huge success. It went beyond being just a consumer promotion to impact the trade especially the retail trade. The price increase also made the distributors happy and support increased, volume sales surged until the factory's full production capacity was utilized and an additional cube couldn't be produced beyond installed capacity. Brand equity was at an all time high, brand name recognition, especially amongst the trade increased, margin was good, and volume was at its highest. The brand had its best year ever. The bold step to do the unthinkable made it happen. It was my best appraisal year as a brand manager in Cadbury, as I broke all the limits.

PLAYING WITH THE GIANTS

Let me share another story to further illustrate the principle of Big Thinking and Big Acting. The biggest global football fiesta, the World Cup, was staged in Africa for the first time in 2010. Historically, global brands were the usual sponsors of the mundial. MTN was at this moment, a regional brand born out of Africa. The brand's ambition was to move beyond being perceived as a regional champion to a truly international brand with fresh perception as a global brand. The world cup was seen by the brand as the singular biggest and most powerful global platform to realize her ambition. The brand therefore chose to join the big league of World Cup sponsors. The brand chose to play with the giants.

The sponsorship investment was huge. The leveraging budget wasn't small either. If you wanted to play in the big league, it became apparent that you had to stretch beyond the small league. Each operating company within the Group was then mandated to ensure a full launch and exploitation of the sponsorship in each country. MTN Nigeria chose to do this in a spectacular way. The world cup was in Africa for the first time. Nobody was sure when the second time would be and so it was a golden moment for brands, soccer enthusiasts and various stakeholders within and outside of government. The strategy was to exploit the power of 'being first' to galvanize the nation around the world cup tournament, offer innovative services built around soccer enthusiasts' passion for the game, and endear the brand to consumers and stakeholders alike. This strategy was given expression in product development, consumer and trade promotions and engagement initiatives between the brand, trade partners, customers and various government and non-governmental stakeholders. The brand made a conscious decision to own a space in the heart of Nigerians as the first brand to give fortunate Nigerians the opportunity to attend their first ever world cup match.

1994 was a watershed in Nigerian football history. The country went to the world cup for the first time. The year is still remembered by many people as the glorious year of Nigerian soccer. To commemorate the World Cup tournament's first time in Africa therefore, MTN Nigeria decided to bring together from across the world, members of the famous 1994 team that took Nigeria to her first World Cup. The reassembled team was then pitched against veterans of African soccer across various countries in Africa in the battle of the giants. The veterans were all brought into Nigeria and made to play together for the first time ever.

These players were flown in from different parts of the world to play the match at the best stadium with a synthetic pitch in Lagos, Nigeria. A world class communication campaign was spun around the match. A consumer promotion was strung around it for active consumer engagement. Various exciting activations were developed around the sponsorship and the stadium was ecstatic. The entire concept and execution was so successful that it became a landmark event in the histories of both the Nigerian marketing industry and the Nigerian soccer universe.

A first-of-its-kind national consumer promotion was also conceived and executed. Winners were offered all expense paid trips to experience the world cup live. Participation was tremendous as the brand's customers seize the opportunity of a lifetime to experience the world cup at no cost at all besides the cost of participation in the promotion.

For the first time in the history of the telecommunication industry in Nigeria, apart from the generic text message based news updates on the tournament, an innovative Value Added Service was developed and launched to generate revenue and further reinforce the brand's innovation and market leadership. This service was a football rich content download. It allowed soccer enthusiasts to download memorable moments like goal moments, memorable

The two teams and their coaches

The game in session

Excited crowd at the stadium

saves, historical defensive moves, etc., onto their phones to be re-played and enjoyed at their leisure. Adoption for this was huge and another 'first' was scored.

The brand crowned these series of leveraging events in Nigeria with the launch of the Guinness Book of World Records accredited biggest soccer ball. This big ball was launched with fanfare and taken round the country on a consumer engagement trip to further reinforce the brand's ambition as a global brand and a world cup sponsor. Monetization and value extraction was integral to all these initiatives, so a tactical consumer promotion was also infused into the Road Show scheme. Participation was tied to Sim and airtime purchase to deepen brand penetration, grow volume and value share, and reward customers.

In the drive to own the innovation leadership platform in the heart of consumers and the nation at large, the brand also innovated the media industry. For the first time in Nigeria, the brand floated giant branded yellow soccer balls on the Lagos lagoon as a means of breaking parity amongst other sponsors represented in Nigeria, and as a new vista in outdoor advertising. The sites were

The Biggest Soccer Ball endorsed by the Guinness Book of world records at set up and during launch

spectacular to behold and altered the marine landscape. No other brand in Nigeria had ever broken clutter in such a differentiated manner until MTN.

Post campaign and post activation research showed that the brand ranked higher than traditional World Cup sponsors in resonance and identification as a sponsor of the FIFA 2010 World Cup, even though the Brand's sponsorship category was lower compared to the traditional global sponsors. The big bold leveraging and value extraction changed the game. Apart from the financial returns from all the value extracting initiatives around products and ser-vices, and the various types of both tactical and national consum-er promotions, these initiatives reinforced the brand's positioning

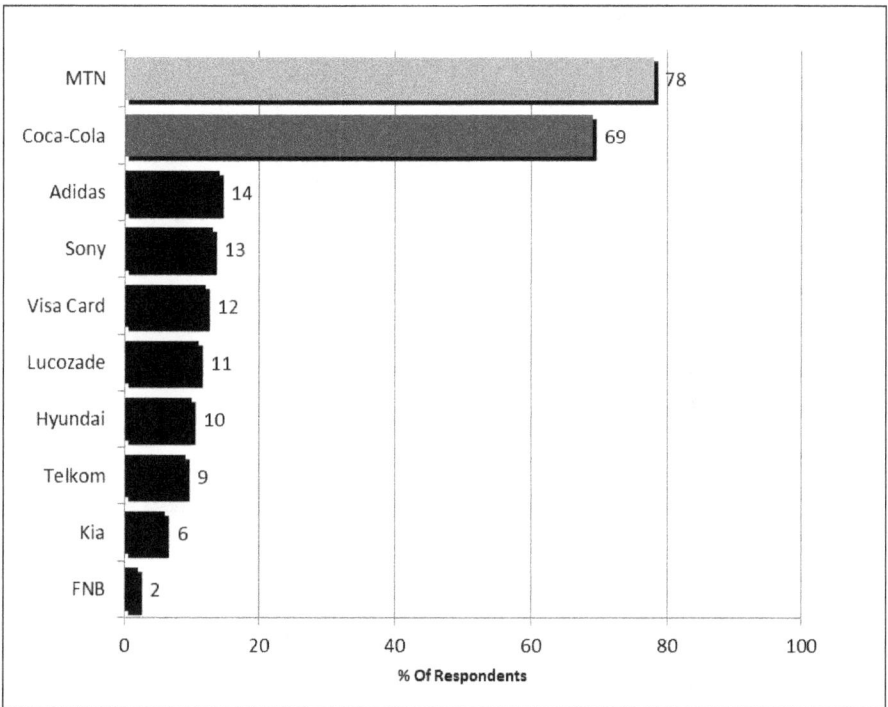

Brand	% Of Respondents
MTN	78
Coca-Cola	69
Adidas	14
Sony	13
Visa Card	12
Lucozade	11
Hyundai	10
Telkom	9
Kia	6
FNB	2

Here, respondents were asked to spontaneously mention all the names of com-panies and brands that they could recall as sponsors of the 2010 Football World Cup. MTN was ahead of the traditional sponsors.

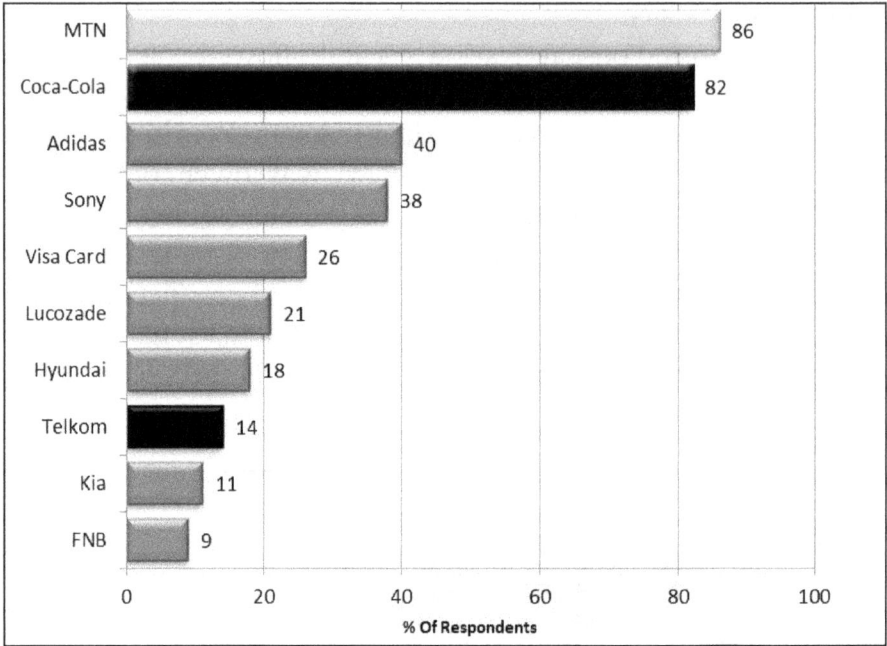

The slide showing the feedback from respondents when they were prompted by a presentation of a list of possible sponsors. They were asked to indicate which of them they believed to be sponsors. MTN still led the traditional sponsors.

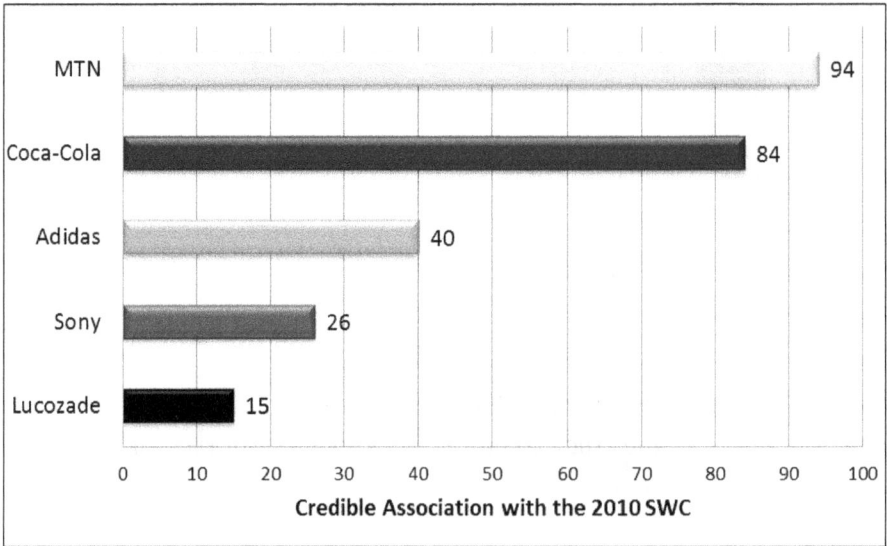

On the issue of credible association with the world cup, the brand still led the pack as seen in the chart.

as both a market share leader and an innovation leader, while also positioning her alongside global brands. Below are some slides showing research data on the post campaign evaluation:

In its overall impact, the world cup provided the MTN Group brand the platform to stand shoulder to shoulder with renowned global brands. The world press covering the world cup and the international community had no choice but to reckon with this young brand born out of Africa with ambitions to play on the global turf. The brand was no longer perceived as a regional brand. It had made the transition into the big league. Locally in Nigeria, the brand's mental, volume and value market share leadership became firmly entrenched, and her preeminent position in the hearts and minds of Nigerians became undisputable.

CHAPTER EIGHTEEN

ATTACK AS THE BEST FORM OF DEFENSE: THE LAUNCH OF MOBILE NUMBER PORTABILITY IN THE NIGERIAN TELECOMMUNICATION MARKET

A surprise attack usually has a devastating effect in war. It shifts the balance of combat power and delivers huge impact at low expense. Shock and confusion are induced and the opposition is caught pants down in its most vulnerable state with huge casualties resulting. This gets even worse when the attack comes from the least expected quarters. In the mobile telecommunication industry, when the regulator introduces the mobile number portability regime, consumers are given the liberty to change their network providers at no cost without losing their numbers. Smaller players are usually more aggressive, because they see this as a window for growth at the expense of the market leader. The usual global trend therefore is that the market leader defends its market share from the invading attackers licensed by the regulator to raid.

The telecommunication regulator in Nigeria introduced the Mobile Number Portability regime in April of 2013 into a four-player market that had the market leader at 46% market share. The market leader not only led in market volume share, the brand was also the market value share leader and had the most number of high value customers in the market. The brand therefore was a very attractive target for porting inducement by the smaller competitors. Porting is the term used to describe the act of changing service provider in a Mobile Number Portability regime.

However, instead of taking a defensive position, the brand chose to go on the offensive. The brand invested in the technical capabilities for number portability and established project teams to manage her readiness for the regime from the moment the regulator announced the Mobile Number Portability agenda and timetable. The project scope was organization-wide and focused on getting every arm of the business ready for the new regime. The objectives were to ensure the brand remained the preferred brand by customers; an attractive destination to port to; and the most technically seamless operator that would make the porting process a painless experience.

Part of the strategy to ensure the brand remained the preferred brand and create further bonding, was to focus on the brand's assets; and tell stories of the brand's impact in the lives of her customers, using the relevant, differentiated and compelling need-based research driven value propositions. The company also focused on leveraging the huge investments it had been making and was still making in the country; the

Taking possession of the material resources and any other resource that strengthens the opposition is a war principle that creates weakness and the disorientation of the opposition. It creates disequilibrium in the opponent's strategy and makes immediate counter-attack difficult.

121

high impact consumer engagement investments in the market through to the corporate social responsibility investments via the MTN Foundation. These were all strategically communicated to the Nigerian public and their impact on national life was given expression.

These strategies were crowned with a bold step to raid one of the competitors by getting a major personality associated with one of the potential aggressors to be the face of the mobile number portability marketing and communication campaign. Taking possession of the material resources and any other resource that strengthens the opposition is a war principle that creates weakness and the disorientation of the opposition. It creates disequilibrium in the opponent's strategy and makes immediate counter attack difficult. MTN did this when the brand signed on a popular icon that had come to embody a particular competitor's brand. This young and aggressive competitor is Etisalat. The campaign was carefully hatched and kept confidential for weeks until the launch of the number portability regime. Its launch was an instant success and it took the center stage in brand discourse, and invaded the media landscape in unpaid-for media mentions across formats and social strata.

This popular icon was engaged by an advertising agency that used to work with Etisalat for a couple of advertising campaigns. This particular agency worked with the actor on a project-by-project basis and did not sign any long-term contract with the actor. Contrary to the public view that the actor was Etisalat's brand ambassador; he was just a model on a tactical basis. This assumption that he was a brand ambassador was occasioned by the success of the campaigns he was used for.

Unfortunately, Etisalat and this agency parted ways, and consequently the actor was left as a free agent at the expiration of the contract he had earlier signed with the disengaged agency. He remained a free agent until the MTN agency team approached him and a deal was struck. He was a perfect fit to communicate the switch to the MTN network by a notable personality from another network. The mobile number portability regime allows competitors to openly prospect one another's customers. It was designed to foster increased competitiveness and offer customers the liberty to move to any network of their choice. Using a personality that had come to be associated with the Etisalat brand as a symbol of a switch to the MTN network was considered a most powerful way to communicate the MTN brand as the preferred network and porting destination.

The resultant advertising campaign was a masterpiece that got the marketing industry, the marketing communication industry, the telecommunication industry and the entire country talking. The advertising copy was simple, yet powerful. The set, props, lighting and entire production values were excellent. The music and its performance by the actor were exciting, yet effective. The campaign was simply powerful. Views on YouTube ran into tens of thousands and Nigerians created their own versions of the dance in a contest to win exciting prizes for the number of likes. Earned media ran into billions of Naira worth of free media mention, and were varied from on-air discussions, press media reviews, analyses by top media personalities to online commentaries and praises for the campaign.

This campaign hit at the heart of Etisalat's strategy, as well as the strategies of the other competitors. As the youngest operator with the desire to capitalize on the mobile number portability regime for growth, the national acceptance of the campaign significantly watered down the impact the brand would have had on the market leader and on the psyche of customers with inclination to port. It threw a credibility punch at the brand. People surmised that if a major icon of the brand could port to competition, then it was a loud encouragement to port from the brand.

The brand fought back in various ways, including complaints to the advertising regulator. Comments on the morality and ethics of the choice of the actor by MTN were raised in different quarters. This discourse became a two edged sword, as it also raised issues about the brand's treatment of the actor when he was with Etisalat. Critics wrote that the relationship with him was not managed well, hence, the man's decision to port to MTN. Some attempts were made to change the conversation via some advertising materials in the press media, imploring people to ignore the MTN advertising and focus on service delivery. This strategy didn't have a bite either, and the general impression was that the organization behind the campaign claiming to be a consumer rights advocacy group was a phantom.

A major lesson from this experience is that brand managers must change their casual approaches to talents engaged in brand marketing and marketing communication advertising productions. We need to develop more strategic long-term relationships. More than ever before, brand managers also need to continuously interrogate the key factors behind propositions and marketing successes. If Etisalat had possibly evaluated the amount of value the actor had added to the brand, and cared, it may have developed a different kind of relationship with him. It probably did not or felt it could do without the value and had to pay dearly for it.

Etisalat and all the potential aggressors like Globacom and Airtel, with plans to grow off the market leader's share hadn't bargained for such an aggressive posture from MTN, the market leader, and so were caught unawares. Their responses to the market were comparatively weak to the market leader and not strong enough to occasion the significant migrations they had envisaged.

In neighboring Ghana, where two of the competitors also play, their responses to the market during the number portability regime in Ghana were very aggressive against the market leader that was incidentally, MTN. They could not achieve the same feat in Nigeria, because MTN went on the attack instead of taking a defensive stance.

The market leader's position was shocking to the entire industry and watered down whatever negative impact the number portability regime could have had on her market share. Instead of losing, the market leader actually gained. MTN led in the share of new connections and saw migrations come in from other networks at the early stage of the regime. The strategy significantly weakened the hands of the smaller operators that could have done damage to the brand's market share. They were not convincing enough to engineer the desired movement against the market leader.

Some critics who did not understand the rationale behind the market leader's strategy criticized the campaign and a particular commentator concluded erroneously that it was a waste of resources. He missed the point. If the brand had stayed in the defense, it would have been badly hurt as the remaining three would have preyed on her, but changing the game made her a net gainer in a regime that would have made her a loser.

NO BUDGET FOR PRISONERS: UNILEVER NIGERIA'S LEADERSHIP OF THE TOOTHPASTE CATEGORY

Still talking about market leaders behaving like challenger brands, the Unilever Nigeria case in the toothpaste category offer good learning. In warfare, holding prisoners is a cost. While it may be a useful strategy to extract strategic information, the cost of maintaining and keeping them alive will exert on the usually limited resources for war prosecution. Global politics even recognizes the rights of prisoners of war. This means budgeting for prisoners! In marketing, where this convention does not hold, marketers hardly hold prisoners. When you have the opposition in retreat, you don't back down. You pursue until you put the enemy to rout. Emotions are not involved; the target is dominance.

Unilever Nigeria gives practical expression to this marketing war principle in her prosecution of market leadership strategies. At over 75% share of the toothpaste market with her CloseUp brand, you would expect that the company would focus on just defending this enviable market share, but Unilever did not. Rather, the company keeps pursuing offensive strategies that have consistently ensured growth and kept competition at bay.

From its launch in 1975, the brand has been driven by parity breaking innovation that eventually saw the brand unseating Macleans; a GSK brand, as the market leader. The managers of the brand did not rest with just becoming the market leader, rather, the brand made total category market development and expansion its mission via new user recruitment and behavioral conversions.

The toothpaste market is divided into the premium, medium and discount segments. The premium segment is made up of imported brands like Colgate and Aquafresh. This segment accounts for a very small share of the market. The medium segment is the largest in share, and is made up of locally manufactured brands like, CloseUp, Macleans and Dabur herbal toothpaste. This segment is medium priced. The discount segment is also made up of imported brands. These are low-end brands like, MyMy and Holdent, and account for a small share. At over 75% share, CloseUp is the biggest masquerade in this category after unseating Macleans as the market leader.

Backed up by relevant data and sound consumer insight, CloseUp has remained the most innovative in this category. From the introduction of variants to new flavours, packaging format and sizes, new market development right up to consumer engagement platforms, the brand has remained at the cutting edge of category redefinition. It's continued market leadership is therefore not accidental. The brand chose to think and act like a challenger in a category where it is the market leader by a wide margin.

The brand developed specific fighter variants to combat competition, while defending her flagship variant. CloseUp Fresh Menthol was developed specifically to attack Macleans and convert loyalists to CloseUp. The brand actually set a target that competition must not grow beyond. The focus is that no matter how large the total market grew, competition must not exceed a certain share. Internally within the company, the CloseUp team strategically pegged Macleans' growth below 5% and executed strategies to ensure this happens. Though strong in the northern part of Nigeria, Macleans was not helped by the limited distribution at pharmacies and grocery stores. Rural penetration was on CloseUp's side.

The brand created and dominated a family health segment with clearly focused sets of strategies. The brand launched a herbal toothpaste variant to develop new users and to fight Dabur; the only herbal toothpaste in the market until the CloseUp variant. A focused attack was launched into the Dabur brand's stronghold in the rural northern part of Nigeria with sampling exercises followed up with sales. Endorsements were secured from health authorities and opinion leaders on the efficacy of the new product. Trade support was huge. Consumer trial was high, and the herbal variant exceeded her volume target within the first year of launch. Developing specific strategies to target brands with 5 and 3 percent shares when you are at a whopping 78 percent share is indicative of a mindset that does not hold prisoners.

Oral health education in schools was given high priority to generate pester effect that can influence purchase. Four hundred and eighty schools, and two hundred thousand students were targeted. Dental students were engaged to give oral health talks, workbooks and cartoons were developed to aid understanding and recall; letters were written to Mums as follow up on the talks, and they were invited to engagement forum with the brand and their children. The talk encouraged morning and evening brushing of teeth as critical to oral hygiene. This automatically means usage growth in an environment where the general belief is that brushing in the morning is good enough oral hygiene. All of these were backed up with above the line marketing communication. The brand leveraged on the end value aspiration of every mother to be seen as a caring mum, who is concerned about the health and well being of her children.

Dominance of key distribution channels with appropriate pack sizes was a major strategic objective for the brand. The brand developed different pack options that ensure penetration and availability at every point of purchase. The brand had open market display contests and Neighborhood shoppers' promotions to drive stocking, display and penetration. While competition had limited distribution, the CloseUp brand had both width and depth.

The brand saw huge opportunities in new market developments. Converting users of the local alternative, chewing stick, was a focused strategy. This category of users were encouraged to try CloseUp, even with their chewing stick initially. This strategy was backed up with growing usage among current users with the 'Twice Daily Brushing' campaign. This was a focused initiative that equated good oral hygiene practice with brushing twice daily: in the morning and at night before bed. Every success here translates directly to volume sales growth.

Focused market development that has grown In-Home-Presence for the brand to 84%. Innovation that saw as much as six different brand innovations within four years, capacity expansion to cater for increased demand occasioned by growth, efficient operational management, value pricing, and a brutal refusal to hold prisoners, have all combined to make this brand the colossus it is in the toothpaste category with about 78% market share.

CHAPTER NINETEEN

THE DEVIL IS IN
THE DETAIL

This is a common saying of mine to my colleagues when planning marketing initiatives and executing strategies. This is because the best strategy can be awfully executed at the risk of the brand's health and the embarrassment of the manager's professional integrity, just by a small error of omission or commission when detailing is not properly done. A tiny detail like not checking that the back-up battery for a projector's remote control is full can mess up a marketing career. The battery can be less than two dollars in cost, but its failure can destroy or sub-optimize a five hundred thousand dollar project. A minor electrical blowout on a microphone can negatively impact sound at a major brand concert, or mess up a brand presentation at a product launch, if there is no back up.

Marketing services suppliers have been fired because generators packed up in the middle of major brand events and venue plunged into total darkness. Brand managers have been queried when masters of ceremonies who were not properly briefed goofed in the recognition of important stakeholders, threw irrelevant banters and cracked inappropriate jokes. Brand equities have been impaired by errors that could have been avoided if proper detailing had been done. The key is to accept the fact that nothing is too small to be ignored when it comes to brand planning and strategy execution.

Smart managers have learnt, and are still learning to scrutinize their project checklist to be sure all areas are covered and back up guaranteed, in case of failures. An area that sometimes escapes scrutiny is in contractual obligations with marketing services suppliers, especially in advertising, media and sponsorships. Globally, sports' marketing is a field that requires, not just marketing skills, but also legal skills. It is a field where you are either, both a lawyer and marketer, or you must hire a lawyer's skills to protect you and ensure that all possible loopholes are covered in your contract to avoid ambush marketing.

MIND THE GAP: BOURNVITA AND NIGERIA '99

Nigeria hosted the Under 17 Junior World Cup tournament in 1999, tagged Nigeria '99. The whole world's attention focused on Nigeria, while the tournament lasted. Coca-Cola was the global sponsor, and so owned the property in Nigeria. All carbonated soft drinks brands were therefore kept out of the possibility of exploiting the huge opportunities for sales, merchandising and direct consumer engagement that the tournament offered.

At this time, I was a young marketing professional with responsibility for the Advertising, Media, Direct Marketing, Sponsorships and Events function for all the brands within the Cadbury Schwepps stable in Nigeria. Bournvita, a cocoa based beverage brand was the company's flagship brand, and a brand marketed on the platform of nutrition, health and wellness, active indoor and outdoor life. The brand had also had a long romance with soccer, having been a sponsor of the country's premier league in the past. In addition to this, Nigeria '99 offered any brand the singular largest gathering of young adult income earners and consumers of various brands. Thus, it was a platform every marketer would have loved to leverage.

We wanted an association with this tournament, but could not do so, due to the huge budget. It was tough to watch the tournament go by with all the opportunities it had and we were helpless. To worsen it, the brand's main competitor seemed to have found a way to still get value from the tournament. Milo was the big bold brand at the entrance to the national stadium, where a considerable number of the tournament's matches held. The brand had the outdoor site well before the tournament, and somehow, managed to hold on to it while the tournament lasted. Brand Bournvita needed to do something.

A breakthrough came when we were approached by an organization that had the rights to host a food, drinks and culture festival within the tournament to promote tourism. It was allocated a very visible space within the stadium complex to host the festival and exhibition. The organization offered us the opportunity to be a part of the festival for a cost that we could afford. This was a huge opportunity and we grabbed it without any reservation. Then, we strategized on how we were going to make our involvement so big it would be difficult for anyone to ignore the brand, despite the small amount of money we paid.

We understood our boundaries and knew we could not visibly identify with the tournament in our communication materials. We were therefore careful not to breach any known law. However, we saw a lot of other opportunities we could exploit for huge returns at minimal cost. Hence, we creatively did a couple of things. We developed a logo that would serve as the arrowhead of our campaign. We couldn't use the Nigeria '99 logo and trademarks, but we created a logo and tagged it 'Football '99'.

Our understanding of the terrain showed that the stadium was in the heart of the city and soccer lovers would have difficulties commuting back and forth on match days, and would also have to deal with traffic jams that could affect their ability to watch the games. We saw an opportunity in this and leased well-maintained commercial buses from the ten seating capacity buses to the fifty seating capacity ones. These buses were branded in Bournvita colours with the Football '99 logo and were positioned at different convergent points in the city to give football lovers free rides to the stadium.

The movements of the buses were coordinated such that they moved in convoys with hazard lights on, to and fro the stadium. Flags of Football '99 were hoisted on the buses. Each bus had a promoter to give brand talks on the journey. Each bus had pre-mixed and chilled Bournvita on board for soccer enthusiasts to sample. Commuters also got free merchandise on board the bus. So, the buses were always full and were a beautiful sight to behold, as they drove from different parts of the city in convoys into the stadium on match days. We extended the Football '99 branding to staff that were excited and offered their cars to be branded. We therefore had moving billboards in different sizes and shapes, from mini buses to large buses and private cars.

At the festival stand within the stadium, we had the full complement of Cadbury brands on exhibition. The company had also just launched Chef Pepper soup Cubes. We got a caterer to make pepper soup with the product for people to sample. Chilled Bournvita was also made generously available for sampling. The combination of chilled nourishing Bournvita to cool down the hot pepper soup, exciting free merchandise, and excellent performances by famous artistes in a relaxed atmosphere within the stadium, made the festival stand very attractive to football lovers, especially when they knew that they could also get a free ride back home. The Bournvita brand had a most rewarding exploitation of the soccer tournament without paying the huge sum that the known sponsors paid.

The main sponsor protested the action and called it guerilla marketing. The main sponsor claimed that even though Bournvita was not a carbonated soft drink, it was still a beverage and a competitor. This may be right and defendable. However, this defini-tion should have been clearly spelt out at the contracting stage to prevent ambiguities. The company that came to Cadbury to offer the deal would have been prevented from talking to any beverage company. Also, if this had been done, the Milo billboard on the main entrance to the stadium would have been taken down while the tournament lasted. It was therefore difficult to claim any legal breach, because the definition of the competitive universe by the main sponsor was exclusive to her, and probably not shared by the organization that sold the rights.

Therefore, it is important to watch out for the details. Get fas-tidious about it even when it sometimes irritates your suppliers. It will save you from avoidable embarrassments. Attention to de-tail is indeed a demonstration of excellent marketing practice. Let your lawyers scrutinize the contracts for deliberate mischief and practiced fraud. Make sure clear service level agreements are enshrined in the contract and penalties for breach clearly spelt out. For consumer engagement projects, draw up a checklist of possible demons to deal with before you step out, and ensure ac-countability on each item. Be clear in allocating responsibilities, and even at the risk of being seen as an irritant, confirm and re-confirm that everything is in place. It is the only way to ensure a faithful delivery of strategy in excellent execution.

CHAPTER TWENTY

PLAYING ON THE EDGE: SOMETIMES, AN APOLOGY WORKS BETTER

This is a piece of advice for marketing or brand managers who want to make a difference. Most folks would rather play safe; but if you want to stand out and excel, you must be daring enough to break some rules. The same principle applies to entrepreneurs who want to make a difference. Playing safe may sometimes not be safe enough to keep you alive in an aggressively competitive world.

In my first year as a full Brand Manager, I was very conscious of the hierarchy and layers of authority required to get approvals before things could get done. I didn't want to rock the boat, and so would diligently prepare my documents and queue up for approvals. These approvals were highly irregular, because of the sheer volume of documents that the then Marketing Manager needed to go through. Sometimes, when you see the Marketing Manager's driver offloading files from the car in the morning, you would wonder if she ever slept. I saw this, felt for her, and was not very aggressive about getting my documents signed off. Then, I got a shocker when I was told during my year-end appraisal that I didn't get those approvals because I wasn't assertive enough. I felt disappointed, but I had learnt my lesson.

The following year, I changed my strategy. I did my homework well, developed a very good relationship with my immediate boss who trusted my capabilities and judgments, and had even told the business earlier that his direct supervision of my function was superfluous. Then, I went to town. I sent in my documents as expected, but did not wait for the approvals before I moved; but I made sure my immediate boss, who had been longer in the business, knew what I was doing. I developed and pursued my brand growth strategy and plans, developed a new brand promise, planned and executed an excellent communication strategy, and executed a high impact consumer promotion.

Getting approval for a new advertising campaign then required approvals from the Product Group Manager, then the Marketing Manager, and finally, the Sales and Marketing Director. These approvals were in two levels after the briefing process: before the production and after the production, before exposure. I broke this rule. I gave approvals right at the agency to ensure campaigns broke on schedule. Initially, my agency was scared, because the folks understood the golden rule on sign-offs for marketing campaigns and were worried that I was breaking them. On a particular occasion, late one night after a TV shoot, my immediate boss and I took a tape straight from the studio to the media house for broadcast, and signed an undertaking to regularize documentation the following day. This was a taboo in the business. We had just broken a golden rule that could cost us dearly. However, we were also aware that delay was dangerous. It was a big gamble against the norms, but a risk required to make a difference.

That same evening, I went back to the office and posted the merchandising materials for the campaign on the doors and the walls of the marketing division. When the marketing manager got into the office the following morning, she went ballistic. I got summoned and queried on why I did what I did without formal approvals. My response was an apology and a statement that my boss was fully aware of what I did. My boss was immediately summoned also and asked to explain himself. He did not refute anything, but calmly apologized and took responsibility. His apology and acceptance of responsibility disarmed the marketing manager, and the excellence displayed in the execution of the project made it difficult to pursue the issue further.

One critical thing to note here is that what we did was not to undermine her authority. Rather, it was a practical solution to an intractable problem of heavy workload that led to slow approvals, and by extension late execution or even non-execution of strategic initiatives. She still got the credit for the success of the entire enterprise. It wasn't about me. It was about getting the job done and staking my professional integrity to make it happen when it mattered.

The consumer promotion and the communication campaign were so successful that the brand sold its highest volume ever that year. Brand equity grew and so did the revenue, because it was a high value, high margin brand. The gamble paid off. The company relished the success. My bosses looked good. Nobody remembered that I broke any rule. The result was more important. The numbers were what counted. I learnt some fundamental lessons from this experience:

1. You never make a difference playing safe
2. It is easier to get forgiveness sometimes than to get approvals.
3. If you would ever succeed as a brand manager or a professional, you need some guts

You never make a difference playing safe. It is easier to get forgiveness sometimes than to get approvals.

and courage to follow your ideas through.

4. Don't be passionately stupid. Exercise your guts only when you have thoroughly done your homework, and then ensure a good understanding of the issues and soundly crafted strategy drives you.

5. Finally, I learnt that a boss with guts and integrity could make a difference to a young manager's career and professional self-esteem. I made up my mind to be one as I grew in my career.

During my appraisal that year, when asked which areas of my person I felt I needed to improve upon, my answer was assertiveness! My boss exclaimed with wonder and asked how else I wanted to demonstrate assertiveness beyond what I had done.

I may have been fortunate to get away with this breach. Some may call it luck; but this is not how it plays out all the time. I have been burnt at different times for daring to exercise initiative. Once upon a time, I had a boss who had very strong contrary views to mine when it came to effective communication and engagement with a particular market segment. He felt we were far too much on the edge and condemned what we believed resonated well with the target. Tried as I could, I couldn't get him to change his mind. Bad politics around him also beclouded his views of my intentions, and he made advertising creative material approval a consensus issue. A large gathering of people, including folks totally ignorant about the advertising development process was made a panel to judge advertising creativity and approve campaigns.

I was worried that the brand was suffering, but was helpless to do anything as whatever I did was seen as an attempt to attract attention to myself. On a few occasions, I took the risk to expose some campaigns without his formal approval. The result was very negative. I got a call one evening about a particular TV commercial that the boss had just seen broadcast. He described it as awful and a waste of money and instructed me to withdraw it immediately. The ad was a very good one that resonated well with the target. However, there was an age difference between the boss and the target, and he unfortunately was viewing the material through his own frame. I gave instructions that the ad should be pulled as directed. However, he rescinded his decision the following day when he got calls from people asking why such an excellent ad that connected well with the target was pulled off.

Therefore, context and personality types can make a difference to how a manager's exercise of intuition and initiative can be viewed and reacted to by superiors and peers. Wisdom demands that young managers get sensitive to these realities. When you are constrained from acting your guts out, don't get discouraged. Keep sharpening your skills and find ways to represent your case where possible. Do not allow the present difficulty to ventilate shut your capacity to think big and act on your guts.

> **Do not allow the present difficulty to ventilate shut your capacity to think big and act on your guts.**

CHAPTER TWENTY-ONE

GET RID OF YOUR BLINKERS: THE ADVERTISING ISN'T MEANT FOR YOU

The heart of a marketer's job is to develop compelling, relevant and appropriately priced propositions based on consumer insights, make them readily available and effectively communicate the same to generate the required consumer action. A key skill set required for success in marketing is therefore effective communication skills, either at inter-personal level or at customer engagement level. You can get the product right. The pricing may be bull's eye and availability may be at every point of purchase. If however you get both the trade and consumer education right, and communication wrong, you can still be a guaranteed failure.

More often than not, brand managers are not the reference targets for the brands they manage. You may be fortunate, maybe once in your life to manage a brand where you are also a reference target. It is hardly the norm. Hence, effective communication with the target requires that you step back from forcing your views and personality on the form and content of the communication to ensure it connects effectively with the target.

However, Brand managers sometimes get too immersed in their intellectual prowess and are blinkered by their biases to the point where they force their personalities on the brand's communication. They sometimes love to see themselves in their ads instead of allowing the target customers to see themselves in the ad. They want ads that please them and reflect their preferences. From the selection of concepts to the choice of story lines, models, producer, location, costume and crew, the brand manager is the selector. He is the professor who thinks and acts for the customer. This is the reason why many creative materials do not resonate with the target customers. The ad was created either for the brand manager or the marketing director.

This gets worse where the client is the owner of the business. The tendency to desire advertising that suits their preferences and makes them feel good is high. Expertise is forcefully subsumed under the bullish power that signs the cheque. Agencies have been known to get fired, just because they refuse to dance to the whims of the almighty client owner of the business. Some get to the point of writing advertising copy and instructing art directions. Advertising agencies that work for such clients are not the enviable stock.

My principle is to ensure that as much as is practicable, the advertising agency communication team reflects where possible, empowered reference consumers, especially when it is a youth brand. Where this is impossible, key members of the team must be immersed in the world of the consumers, so they can have a first hand understanding of the taste and preferences of the consumer. You can only connect with consumers when you understand the dynamics behind their choices, motivations, consumption habits and purchase decisions. To do this successfully, you are either one of them or you've chosen to learn from them.

In my early days as an advertising practitioner, I worked on a brand of sanitary pad, and was part of the team that launched it into the Nigerian market. The brand believed in the strength of a proprietary technology that prevented leakages from normal or heavy menstrual flows. Practical demonstrations, product placements, and comparative analysis were the platforms the brand pushed in its communication to show its superiority over competing brands and local substitutes.

As an executive working on this brand, despite my gender, the brand manager and I were made to go round the country listening to women describe their experiences during menstruation. We found out what the women used during their menstrual periods and gave them samples of the brand to try. We later went back to learn what their experiences were and sought insights into what their core needs were and how the needs were either met or unmet when they used the brand. We also sought for information on how the brand compared with competition, and whatever else the women were used to before they came in contact with the brand.

Initially, the women were uncomfortable with a man around, but soon got used to me, and were very free to speak without any restraint. During these immersion sessions with the consumers, I learnt the various forms of emotions associated with menstruation periods. I understood the various options ladies use, their efficiencies, limitations, and most of all the hygiene issues surrounding the various options.

I heard and learnt so much that I could write a book on menstruation and women hygiene. The resultant communication used actual words and expressions that women used to describe their feelings whenever they used either the brand or the options provided. It connected with women and the brand was a success. Immersion in the consumer's world, and not just immersion in the brand made the difference. The brand believed in it and invested in it. The result could not be faulted when the knowledge was correctly applied.

However, we are in an age where clients either force themselves on the creative process or advertising practitioners create adver-

> **If we understand that the brand is the business, we may probably be a lot more careful in foisting our sentiments on the communication process. We must remember that the advertising is not meant for us. It is meant for the reference customer. If we happen to be one, it is purely coincidental.**

tising from brochures and brand information booklets without an exhaustive understanding of the brand and its consumers. Capturing authentic consumer emotions that can serve as the bedrock of effective advertising that resonates with the target customer is left to the whims or creative ingenuity of the business owner or the robustness of the imagination of the copywriter.

There was a classic case of a Marketing Director who spoke English as a second language. He had resumed in the organization at a point when a new television commercial had just been shot for a project. He condemned the commercial and asked for it to be re-edited to suit his understanding. The end result was a long winding bland commercial that struck no chord with the target. Nevertheless, he was delighted that his preferences ruled the day and couldn't appreciate the divergent views. The brand is usually the loser in such circumstances. We must be humble enough to step back and let the consumer be the hero.

An advertising agency once had an interesting engagement with a marketing director who had authorized a particular television commercial to be shot, but changed his mind mid-stream when it was too late to correct anything. The agency believed in the commercial and attempted to get a change of position, but failed. This agency then took the risk to expose the advertising at its own cost in a small market and got a resounding positive feedback. The problem was that while they got professional satisfaction that they had done a good job, they couldn't share the result with the client, because of the fear of being seen as rebellious and antagonistic to the marketing director's position. The agency had to be contented in the fact that the advertising won her an industry recognized award. Though, the brand was still the loser. If we understand that the brand is the business, we may probably be a lot more careful in foisting our sentiments on the communication process. We must remember that the advertising is not meant for us. It is meant for the reference customer. If we happen to be one, it is purely coincidental.

CHAPTER TWENTY-TWO

WHEN TO COPY
IS WISDOM

Innovation leadership is paranoia for many brands. They are driven by the passion to be the first in developing new products and services and so invest heavily in research and development. This is great as a differentiation platform and an avenue for organic growth via cross-selling, deep selling or up selling of value adding services or variants of the original product. Fantastic brand extensions and new brands have developed from such investments by companies. However, some other brands do not care at all. They invest minimally in research and development, and just wait for competing brands within the category to make the major investments. They simply pick up the innovations, enhance them, mass-produce and use route to market, effective consumer education, effective communication and affordable pricing to drive adoption. Sometimes they do it so well that consumers are left confused about who invented the service. These brands are not ashamed to copy. It's a strategic choice defined as 'smart'.

Interestingly, some brand managers refuse to copy, more out of pride than the passion to be different, or a commitment to out-perform competition on innovation. This is foolishness from my perspective. There are certain industries where refusal to copy is sheer stupidity. In a commoditized industry where parity can be gotten on all the levers of proposition development in days, and the cost of change or churn is low, refusing to copy can kill the brand. The consumer here is not so loyal. He is a bargain hunter and cannot be trusted. He is constantly comparing prices and crisscrosses carpets based on offers from any of the competing brands.

Such an industry is mobile telecommunication. In Nigeria, this industry's competitive levers have demonstrated an interesting cyclical dimension as in the diagram below:

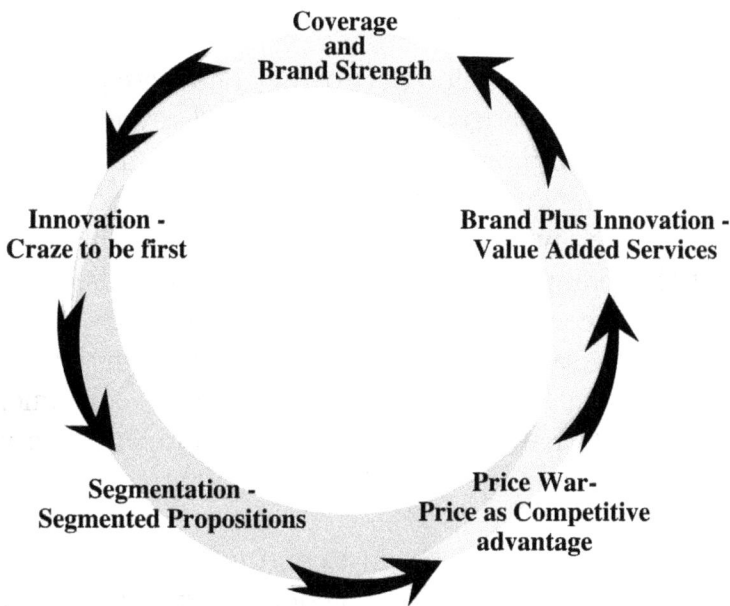

**Coverage
and
Brand Strength**

**Innovation -
Craze to be first**

**Brand Plus Innovation -
Value Added Services**

**Segmentation -
Segmented Propositions**

**Price War-
Price as Competitive
advantage**

At inception, the determinants of choice were coverage and brand strength driven by pedigree and to some extent, the international cues the brands exuded. Image advertising to establish gravitas and evoke emotions of credibility, scale and capabilities combined with educational materials on coverage footprints ruled the communication landscape in the industry.

Innovation was the next competitive frontier. Brands managers battle to claim who launched which initiative first. Claims of 'another first from', 'the first from' and 'the only network with' filled the landscape as brands battle for market leadership perception. The battleground later shifted to segmented value proposition development and data capacity and capabilities. Parity was however quickly achieved here, and brands just replicated competitive proposition packages in whatever forms with minor tweaks.

In a particular instance, a brand copied a competitor's proposition within forty-eight hours of release, including the errors made in the communication of the proposition packages. It was comical, but revealed the extremely short turnaround time to achieve parity.

This was followed by a value-destroying era, where price became the most visible competitive tool before brand strength, data coverage, and innovation returned as competitive levers. Pricing as a destructive tool however overrode any of the earlier choice determinants for a long while, and the industry became fully commoditized. At this point, no brand could ignore price-offs, discounts, and the new 'freemium' economy forced brands to struggle to outdo one another in the amount of freebies they can throw at the customers. The only short-term winner here is the consumer who is wise enough to have the Sim cards of all competing networks and could take advantage of all offers without stress.

This is a two edged sword, because continued investments in the networks by shareholders demand continued positive returns. A lower return on increasing investments, which is what the freemium economy delivers, makes continuous investment unattractive. Refusal to invest impacts the quality of service, as usage grows at low margins. Poor network services will at the same time attract complaints from the same group of customers. This becomes a vicious cycle that is not sustainable. It's a cycle that needs to be broken to preserve the industry. It's an industry that does not obey natural business laws. When there is pressure on margins naturally, businesses explore price increment as a strategy, in addition to other cost cutting strategies.

However, the reverse is the case in the Nigerian telecommunications industry. Just as pressure increases to depress margins from increased cost of service delivery, the market also demands for price reductions. Hence, the business is squeezed at both ends. This is dangerous and unsustainable, and if not stemmed, will ultimately make the industry unattractive. Tragically, competitors are still driven by volume market share grab, instead of migrating to the value share terrain, so that average margins per user becomes the universal metric for measuring performance.

One of the key reasons why achieving parity in this industry seems so easy except in the areas of customer service, route to market, Go To market strategies and efficient internal processes, is the fact that all operators shop from the same mall for their hardware and software. The industry has the same equipment manufacturers, the same value added service developers and vendors, the same consultants, the same market structure, and to some extent, the same customers. Coverage is one factor that may give operators some competitive advantage for a considerable period of time. This is because of the challenges of the long lead time it takes to sort out equipment order, delivery and clearing, several legislative and regulatory bottlenecks to obtaining approval for right of way to lay cables, site acquisition, site construction time, and a host of other environmental and regulatory issues. However, these are not insurmountable in record time. Parity here is also a matter of time.

In an industry like the one described above, it is not so wise to take an arrogant stance of 'No Copy'. I would rather advocate for smart copying when necessary. Pick the innovation, improve on it, tweak it to give it your unique flavor, and hit the market powerfully with excellent communication of the same in double quick time to prevent the customer migrations that freebies occasion.

Though, the cycle of choice determinants closes as customers discover that practically all the operators are offering the same

147

thing from coverage, to innovations, value proposition packages, discounts, etc., the wheel turns right back to the strength of the brand and its evocations. Brand value and innovation leadership communication to occupy an emotional high ground in the mind of consumers becomes increasingly important. Brand affinity and loyalty drivers begin to command focus, as the wheel closes. Any brand that must succeed in this category must recognize these evolutions and evolve alongside.

In conclusion therefore, differentiation is critical to marketing success, and by all means, differentiate on all possible fronts from product concepts to pricing models, route to market structure, go to market strategy and communication. However, if you find yourself in a commoditized category competing against irrational competitors, it is wisdom to copy when you have to. Innovation is not just about doing new things. It is also about doing old things in a new way. When there is a need to, shorten the development turnaround time and needless investments. Pick up an innovation by your competitor, enhance it, brand it uniquely yours, and take it to market in a disruptive way. If you do it well, the consumer may even reward you with the tag of the original inventor.

CHAPTER TWENTY-THREE

HIRE A MIXED MULTITUDE

A brand managerial role is a leadership function. In a proper marketing orientated company, the Brand manager is like a General Manager with an end-to-end oversight over his brand from input to output. A brand manager is not a communications manager, even though he must be an effective communicator. He is a business manager.

A brand is a tactic of business, and the brand manager has a responsibility to deliver specific financial numbers as enshrined in the organization's business plan for the financial year. Regardless of his level within the organization, the brand manager wields a lot of influence across the business as he is empowered to engage with every level of the company hierarchy to ensure his brand's numbers are delivered. From the research and development laboratory to the factory floor; from inbound logistics to inventory control and outbound logistics; from a full understanding of the commercial function of product line costing to trade structure and profitability analytics; from advertising development to media management; from public relations management to sponsorship and events, a brand manager is expected to know enough about a lot to be a generalist, and to know a lot about some things to be a specialist or an expert. He must also possess sterling leadership qualities to provide direction to teams he may not have a direct

Successful brand management therefore, requires a significant level of lateral thinking. It is not just about the numbers. Even though logic crunches and calculates the numbers, magic makes the numbers a reality. Magic makes them happen.

supervisory role over, or even teams made up of his superiors.

From this rough job description, it is clear that marketing is a mixture of logic and magic. Number crunching, data analysis, profitability calculations and projections, all reside in the logic realm. Leadership skills, emotional intelligence, Product concept development, advertising creative development and sponsorship, and events management skills, all reside in the magic realm. Successful brand management therefore requires a significant level of lateral thinking. It is not just about the numbers. Even though logic crunches and calculates the numbers, magic makes the numbers a reality. Magic makes them happen.

When taking a hiring decision therefore, as a senior marketing person or as a business manager, hire a mixed grill. Hire a combination of logical and lateral thinkers. Unfortunately, we tend to hire folks like us or folks we find amenable to cloning. There is hardly any room for contrarians. Great marketing teams are not made of folks who think alike. They are made of folks so passionately diverse in their thinking that they spark beautiful fires of creativity.

I deliberately encourage divergence in my team, but insist that at the end of every brainstorming session, our divergence must converge to actionable strategies that must be flawlessly executed. I expect everyone in my team to have an opinion on issues and insist that such opinions get shared when we are discussing such issues. People are free and encouraged to disagree in professionally polite ways. Young managers can take on their seniors strategically. My sessions are no holds barred sessions without any rudeness or fear of recriminations. We take polite jabs at one another. My managers enjoy it when the joke is on me and know it is nothing personal. They also know I am capable of giving good jabs. We operate as a family, but fight as often as is required in the pursuit of delivering on our targets.

This is possible only because we are so different from one another, and at the same time so comfortable with one another to sit in a room, lock the door and turn our differences into a formidable force for success. I have folks with backgrounds in economics, engineering, statistics, finance, liberal arts, and technology, with all their idiosyncrasies in my team. Their knowledge and experiences were very diverse before they chose marketing as a career. Were we to all be the same, our thinking would have been too boringly similar and unable to create the creative fireworks required to win in the market place. For me, diversity in backgrounds, knowledge, gender, race, ethnicity and faith is a great asset in a marketing team.

HIRING AN AGENCY-HIRE AT LEAST YOUR CEREBRAL EQUALS

This is one of the most important responsibilities of a brand manager or marketing director. Once the brand management team has successfully developed a compelling and relevant value proposition based on sound insight, communicating this proposition to the trade and the consumer is the next critical job. The best of propositions can fail if wrongly communicated. Thus, the choice of the right advertising agency as a partner is very important. If you get the hiring decision wrong, you can compromise the fortunes of the brand.

The process of conducting advertising agency pitches can be very unnerving depending on the size of the account. The stakes are usually very high and emotions run deep. I find this particular portion of the marketing profession very challenging given the Nigerian environment where there is a general, but erroneous belief that merit has no place; only political networks, connections and money rules. It gets worse when it is a mega account that can determine the survival or demise of an incumbent agency. Sometimes, these stakes are so high and the terrain so treacherous that as process midwives, it can endanger your career.

Brand managers enjoy calling the shots and so generally prefer agencies populated by executives that defer to them. These imbue a feeling of power and invincibility in brand managers. Sometimes, when you hear a brand manager speak to an agency executive, you marvel at the bullying that goes on. One of the motivations that propelled my desire to practice core marketing management was that I felt this bullying first hand in my early days as a young advertising executive.

In those days, clients were revered somewhat. When the leadership team of the client company indicated a visit to the agency, everyone was demanded to be in the best behavior. When you are at a meeting and you hold divergent views with the client, you are careful how you express them without offending the almighty client. As a young executive, you watch your boss' body language and conform to the prevailing culture. Then clients carried themselves like kings and demonstrated profound knowledge about their brands, the consumers and the market. Many of us assumed this demonstration of knowledge equated superiority of intelligence, until situations proved otherwise.

Two bullying experiences remain indelible in my memory. As an advertising agency executive, one of the earlier training and discipline you get is how to write Contact Reports. This is a very important document that captures discussions and decisions taken at the meetings with the client. It details the actions required, the timing and who was responsible. By the rule then, this was meant to be circulated maximum forty-eight hours after the meeting. It usually was a tough one for young executives, especially if the meeting was long and you wanted to actively participate. You were compelled to contribute to the discourse on the sideline, and yet listen in on everybody's contribution, so you can effectively summarize the proceedings and the output. I hated this part of the job.

Sometimes, these meetings run till late at night, but you must stay back to put your contact report together, so you don't miss the elements, get it typed and corrected by your boss, and send out to the client. We had a particular client who took delight in aggravating my pain and hatred for writing contact reports. At the next meeting when you should review the status of this report with this client, he will pick the envelope, squeeze it and throw in the thrash can in your presence. If you protested, he would retort that what you wrote in the unread report was your view and ask you if you wanted to continue the meeting or not. You cannot imagine how many times I felt like punching him in the nose. However, I couldn't do anything and my company insisted that I continued writing the contact report. What a pain it was!

Another client once walked my team leader and I out of his conference room, because my team leader had the effrontery to challenge him on some issues. I felt disgusted with this particular client, because a few months earlier, I was part of the agency team that inducted him into the basics of the marketing communication practice when he was hired. It was an infuriating insult, but even though we could protest his behavior, it wouldn't have withdrawn the insult.

From this point on, I began to nurse the desire to get into full marketing practice, because I didn't see myself with the capacity to continue with the insults into adulthood. Then came my big break that demystified clients. I went on training at a business school, and I was in class with some 'almighty' clients. I discovered that the knowledge they demonstrated about their brands, market and consumer was a function of the access they had to information that was sometimes proprietary. I saw that they were not more intelligent than I was. In fact, I found out that I was faster on the draw than a number of them. That did it for me. I knew that all I needed too was access to information. I knew that with the same level of access to information, I was going to excel in marketing practice.

Till date, I hate bullying and see bullies as unprofessional. You can be assertive and get results without being obnoxious. I also believe that robust debates that deliver exceptional performance is impossible if your partners are not, at least, your cerebral equals. Therefore, I do not advocate the hiring of agencies that are susceptible to bullying, either because of their real or perceived intellectual weakness, or because they did not get the business on merit. When managing the advertising agency hiring pitch process therefore, I am more concerned about hiring a partner that will be an asset to me, and not a liability that my team and I can bully.

Your cerebral equals will make the marketing job exciting. They offer you perspectives that you may be blind to. They engage you and stimulate your thinking. They may come across sometimes as difficult or opinionated, but if you look beyond their human limitations, they can make a great team. I have had causes to insist on certain hiring decisions by my agency, because of the intellectual firepower I see in certain individuals, and have had occasions to get my agency to retain people just for the same reason of the level of value they add to intellectual discourses on the brand. I love intellectual engagements and look for the capacity in my partners.

I do not believe you should allow extraneous factors to force you into hiring an agency that will be an intellectual liability on you. If you do, it will come back to haunt you. You will not only define your brand and communication strategy, you will also be the one to define the creative strategy, write the copy, suggest the art direction, supervise production and plan your media. It is not a wise route to travel.

CHAPTER TWENTY-FOUR

ADVERTISING THAT SELLS: BETWEEN ENTERTAINMENT AND FUNCTIONALITY

As an advertising agency executive early in my career, I was part of a team that shot what we considered an excellent TV commercial for a cough syrup brand. The concept leveraged on the renowned affinity between fathers and daughters. It was a beautiful commercial that was well directed and paraded excellent models that dramatized the benefits of the brand effectively well. Industry colleagues applauded. Even the media gave positive reviews. The brand management team from the company was excited. The agency team felt good. This excitement was however short lived.

We got a call from the company's country manager about four weeks into the campaign, and he asked both the brand management and advertising agency teams what we felt about the advertising. Of course, both teams were full of praises for the advertising and cited feedbacks to corroborate our positions. The gentleman allowed us to revel in our excited state before he threw the bombshell.

He looked at us with a smile that was at absolute variance with his next statement. 'Guys, we have to kill this advertising. Its not working', he said, still with a smile across his lips. We all went on

The commercial environment requires a different kind of creativity. It is creativity that sells and not just entertains.

the defensive and began to advance various reasons why we believed his verdict was wrong. Like a good leader that he was, he allowed us to ventilate and unburden our minds of all possible reasons why he may be wrong. Then he said to us, 'Guys, you are getting emotional'. This is not an emotional issue. The cash register is not ringing'. He then shared some numbers with us and instructed that the advertising be rested for a more effective one, because it wasn't making the expected difference to the bottom line. This was my first baptism into a school of advertising that focuses on a balance of functionality and entertainment value.

Sometimes, advertising agency writers focus on winning awards instead of delivering on the commercial objectives of campaigns. A lot of creative departments are populated by creative writers who will do excellently well in the theatre or movie industries, but who are colossal failures as commercial creative writers. After a very frustrating experience on a particular project, I made a very angry remark about a piece of work by a writer in a particular agency. The account manager played back what I said to the writer verbatim. She was so infuriated to the point that she couldn't hide her fiery anger when she saw me afterwards. She went screaming at me; 'I hate you. I hate you'. I understood her tantrums and was not offended at her anger. It is a natural feeling amongst writers and creative people generally. They feel very paternal with their works and take negative comments very personal. I smiled and took time to explain to her the difference between what she was doing and what was needed. She grudgingly accepted my explanation with a lot of pacifiers, shrugged and walked off.

The truth is that this particular writer was very creative. Her work was however better suited for the theatre or the movie industry. The commercial environment requires a different kind of creativity. It is creativity that sells and not just entertains. She needed to understand that my challenge was not on the question of whether she was creative; rather, it was the kind of creativity. She has since followed her passion for the theatre. I have been to see her production and it was outstanding. Had she remained in advertising without a re-orientation, she would have become frustrated or become an expert at entertaining commercials that don't sell.

In the early days of a brand of sanitary pads in Nigeria, the television commercials were very functional and effective at selling the superior technology behind the product and the attendant benefits in the brand promise. However, they were very predictable with little or no entertainment value. Once you've seen them once, you don't look forward to seeing them again, because there was nothing entertaining about the advertising. This brand has since changed into a lifestyle brand and has injected some entertainment value into its communication. The clinical, purely functional communication style is the other extreme side of the pole.

I am an advocate of the ABS principle. 'Always Be Selling' is a maxim with me. Selling here does not mean retail price communication alone. It is the sale of whatever communication message content the brand sets out to pass across to the end consumer. At the end of the commercial, the consumer should not be left thinking or asking; 'what's in this for me?' It should have been evident in the advertising message.

Advertising creative people can be very opinionated and close-minded sometimes. They get very paternal about their art and take any criticism of their brainchild as an affront that must be resisted with linguistic violence where physical violence is unpopular. I was a guest lecturer at an advertising industry seminar on creativity, and after talking extensively about commercial creativity to practitioners, a practitioner in the class vigorously took me on that I was advocating the destruction of their art with my focus on the need to sell. His reaction was indicative of his advertising school. What he failed to realize is that he could cost his agency a very good account, if he focuses on writing advertising that pleases his creative ego.

Entertainment is good, but is useless if it is at the expense of the brand message. Extreme focus on functionality is also limited. Consumers will use the power of the remote control to rid themselves of your advertising if they are boring and uninspiring. A balance is what is desirable. Entertain the consumer enough to keep his attention, so he is put in a state where you can dramatize your brand message to him effectively. This aids recall and engenders a desire to want to see the advertising over and over. In this instance, the almighty remote control will work in your favour.

Some have argued that short retail advertising focusing on prices or promotions cannot be creative or exciting. I once entertained this wrong notion too, but not anymore. Experience has proven to me that the imagination of the brand team and the creative writer is the limitation. A good dose of creative ingenuity combined with an exploratory open mind can make anything happen.

The industry challenge is mostly rooted in the recruitment and training process for creative writers. There is nothing wrong in recruiting talents in creative arts, literature and English studies as writers. However, this does not mean great writers can only emerge from this group. There are folks who never had any creative or liberal arts background, but who are ingenious at unbundling issues and creatively capturing the most important elements of a discourse in very short powerful words that tell the story effectively. When such minds are trained to spin commerce into their creativity, they become advertising geniuses.

Relevant and effective training for writers straight out of school on how to turn their art into commercially relevant art is important for the enlargement of the creative talent pool. Where this training is missing, mediocrity will fester. Functionally useless, but entertaining advertising that waste resources will become the norm. You can have a boardroom full of advertising industry awards on creativity; they may not help you much. What will keep your business growing and generate referrals for you are awards from brands you have helped to grow into market leaders and global brands. This does not happen accidentally. You have to create the structure, the system and the environment to make it happen.

This is a two way street. The brand management team too must be open minded enough to explore when the advertising creative team pushes the frontiers of creative ingenuity to create great advertising that sells. If the brand management team is furtive, staid or loves playing safe, parity breaking effective advertising that entertains and sells simultaneously may be impossible. The two teams must work together. I am a firm believer that a client is as good as the advertising he gets. An endorsement of a piece of advertising for exposure is a statement on the brand manager or marketing director's competence. His professional integrity is behind it.

CHAPTER TWENTY-FIVE

SPONSORSHIPS, EVENTS, AND BRAND ENDORSEMENTS

I was a speaker at the first Nigerian Entertainment Conference, and while discussing the relationship between the corporate world and the entertainment industry, an interesting debate ensued. Practitioners in the entertainment industry believed that corporates were parasitic and only feed on the products of the entertainment industry without any desire to genuinely invest in the industry. I deferred from the promoters of this point of view, not just because I represented corporate Nigeria at the event, but because I genuinely believed that they were not totally correct.

Before this period in question, I had personally been privileged to have at various times, initiated and/or supervised significant brand investments in projects that discovered rookies and raw talents, groomed them and gave them platforms for self expression, recognition and stardom. I was also aware of a couple of other brands that had made similar investments both locally and internationally. It was therefore difficult for me to agree with the proponents of parasitic relationships. These proponents believed that the engagement of popular stars by brands was wrong and exploitative, because they believed that such brands did not contribute to the emergence of such stars. Neither did the brands contribute in any way to the industry that produced such stars from their perspective.

From the deep passion the protagonists of the school of parasitic relationship exhibited in advancing their arguments, I could see that the people were sincerely wrong. I surmised that a significant number of practitioners in the entertainment industry did not appreciate why brands get involved in customer engagement initiatives like Sponsorships and Events. I also saw a misunderstanding of the reasons why brands engage popular icons, stars and celebrities for marketing campaigns and endorsements. We will attempt some clarifications here.

Brands are not charities or Foundations that are not for profit. Marketing budgets are specifically meant for well-defined financial objectives, such as growth in volume and value market share, share of new users, brand equity and retention. Hence, the Periscope brand managers use for evaluating project proposals is totally different from the type used by the Corporate Affairs managers or managers involved in managing corporate social responsibility portfolios, even though they are symbiotic.

Secondly, the primary concern of brand managers is not to develop other industries. When developments occur, it means such an industry is within the brand management ecosystem and simply benefited from the brand's value creation process. However, when ancillary industries expect deliberate investment by brands for supposedly altruistic purposes, such expectations are mis-

The primary concern of brand managers is not to develop other industries. When developments occur, it means such an industry is within the brand management ecosystem and simply benefited from the brand's value creation process.

placed. Marketing budgets are allocated for clear business objectives, and not to champion the cause of ancillary industries.

Brands also strategically engage icons within the music, sports and movie industries as brand ambassadors or to endorse their brands. The relationship here must be symbiotic. The icon must possess some values that are in sync and will help to further promote the brand's values. The brand and the icon must both benefit from the deal. The icon adds value to the brand, while the icon benefits in handsome financial returns. Value is the name of the game here, not emotions about the origin of the icon.

Sponsorships and Events properties revolve around the entertainment world of music, movies, sports and fashion. Brands engage in the sponsorship of properties in these areas with clear intentions to use these passion point platforms to engage their customers as rewards for loyalty, for product launches, sales, and sometimes, to excite customers and the market. Rigorous evaluations along the line of financial and non-financial benefits are done for every property to ensure that the inherent leveraging windows are fully exploited where they exist, and the property either dumped or enhanced where the leveraging opportunities are marginal or nonexistent. New schools of thoughts are emerging and measurement metrics and models are becoming increasingly more popular in this field.

> **Brand equity and affinity building are no longer good enough as justifications for investments in sponsorship properties. The Chief Finance Officers in organizations recognize and respect numbers, not prose**

162

Organizations are more demanding and greater scrutiny is being paid to investments in sponsorships and events. Brand equity and affinity building are no longer good enough as justifications for investments in sponsorship properties. The Chief Finance Officers in organizations recognize and respect numbers, not prose. Arguments that significant portions of brand management investments do not deliver instant hypodermic syringe effect have been advanced, challenged and debated. The grammatical eloquence of brand managers has failed to adequately answer the practical questions of value when decisions on sponsorship property investments are to be taken, if numbers are not involved. This has had positive effects to the end that today, analytic tools have been developed to measure returns on investment where it is possible to have tangible financial returns, and return on objectives for areas where immediate financial returns cannot be calculated. This is a major shift from the old school.

There is a value circle of impact model that clearly shows how well thought through sponsorship properties deliver value based on a full exploitation of inherent or augmented leveraging opportunities. These four value circles of impact are as seen in the diagram below:

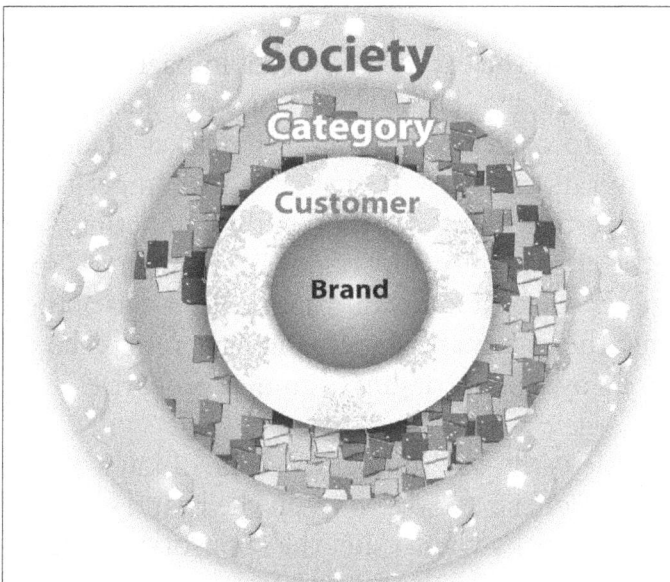

Diagram

At the heart of this model is the brand itself. This analyses the impact of the sponsorship property directly on the brand funding it. Analyses on actual sales, number of sales leads generated, significance and value of attendees as sources of research information and feedback generation for new products, impact of platform for product launches, potential of attendees for sampling purposes, up selling, deep selling and cross selling opportunities, plus actual pitches showing number of closures where possible, brand equity and affinity building opportunities, and customer delight and retention potential, all gets done here. This process is internal to the brand. It is very scientific and reduces guesswork to a very low degree.

The immediate circle of impact close to the brand is the customer circle of impact. How did the property make the customer feel? Did it promote the customer's passion or help him in the enjoyment of his passion? Was it strong enough to make him more loyal to the brand? Did it turn him into an advocate for the brand? Did it engender a conversion where a non-user was targeted? These questions can only be answered via research. On the spot data gathering, as well as post event back-check to seek for short or medium term resonance is therefore important.

The third circle is the category circle of impact. This looks at the competitive terrain and how the property in question has helped or may help to confer mental and or market leadership to the brand within its category. It evaluates its competitiveness with similar properties being sponsored by competing brands, and analyses the opportunity cost of not investing in the property. It also evaluates the cost and value derivable in the proposed property against the cost that competition pays versus the value it derives from its own sponsorship of similar properties.

The last circle is the environmental circle of impact. This checks for the impact of the sponsorship on the brand's operational environment. It checks what value the sponsorship adds to the society, ancillary industries and the possibility of a corporate so-cial responsibility value-adding window. This indicates how the sponsorship may help to develop an entire ecosystem around the brand's marketing management initiatives. Emotional equity op-portunities are explored here to stretch the value of the sponsor-ship beyond fundamental marketing objectives.

Any sponsorship property that returns a net positive result based on this analysis requires only one last thing: execution excellence. No matter how brilliant the output of the analysis, if execution is poor, it is a waste and can sometimes be significantly counterpro-ductive to the brand's health.

CHAPTER TWENTY-SIX

DEVELOPING MARKET LEADERSHIP

Market leadership is a conscious and strategic decision, planned for and excellently executed. It is not an accidental occurrence, but the end product of a series of well-crafted incidents. A brand can desire or wish for market leadership, but until the wish is translated into sound actionable strategies, it will remain just a wish. A brand is a tactic of business. Thus, decisions for market leadership by brands do not start with the brand, they start with the business. The foundation is ingrained in the business strategy where a conscious strategic choice on where and how the organization wants to compete is made. It's the point at which the business determines if it wants to compete for volume or value. Straddling the divide is risky and may lead to brand failure.

Once the business has made the strategic choice on where and how it wants to compete, then we can get down to the brands it chooses to fight with. The first area of leadership that any brand that wants to be a market leader must focus on is in understanding the consumer better than competitors. Insight is the bedrock of sound strategy. Insight informs the brand's ability to develop differentiated, relevant and compelling value proposition packages that consumers will try, purchase, and develop loyalty for.

Quite a number of brands pay lip service to the issue of consumer insight. Rooms and hard drives filled with data do not translate to insights. Weekly, monthly, and even daily tracking studies do not equate to insight. It is beyond data. It is deeper than basic analytics. Few brands have developed and perfected the skill set and techniques for extracting insights from raw data. Brands that do this well are better positioned to begin the journey to market leadership by using the insights to develop propositions, define innovative routes to market and high impact consumer engagement strategies.

Market leadership demands that the managers of such brands are visionary. They must see the role of the brand beyond just selling volumes or making huge margins. There must be a bigger goal that is transformational and beyond the immediate gratification of volume and value numbers. It must have a philosophy that is greater than the financials, but which ultimately guarantees the financial into the long term. This big vision when pursued makes the brand integral to the life of the consumer and elevates the brand's consumer discourse and relationship beyond the mundane.

Brands focused on market leadership are not weak brands and are not managed by weaklings. Managing for market leadership demands courage and boldness to thread where other brands are afraid to venture. The brand must be daring enough to chart new courses, challenge the norms, and push the frontiers of tradition. It must not be risk averse and the managers must be disciplined risk takers. If a brand is too safety conscious, the likelihood of market leadership is nil.

Investment choices require a lot of courage and guts. This is especially true in the developing economies where uncertainty is the only certainty. The risk of losses due to an unstable polity or irrational government policies is usually high. For instance, research information showed that when MTN took the decision to invest in Nigeria in the early years of the country's fledgling democracy when nobody was sure that the army would not come back, it was seen as an insane decision. The stock market's reaction in South Africa was negative. The share price was negatively impacted when the decision became public, but a few years down the line, the story changed when the risk paid off. The brand's decision and success story has since emboldened other global brands to invest in Nigeria.

I had the opportunity of being at a telecommunication conference in Cape Town, South Africa once, and a senior manager in a Nigerian bank almost slapped an industry analyst that had predicted that the Nigerian market was too volatile for investments and warned prospects about investing in the Nigerian telecom industry. Unfortunately for the leader of the firm of industry analysts, he was now at this particular conference eulogizing MTN and its success story when the banker took him on. The anger of the banker was palpable. It was apparent that his company had held back from investing in the Nigerian telecommunication industry based on the analyst's report. His bank was scared to take the risk and so lost the opportunity to partake in the success story. MTN did. The brand dared to invest in Nigeria when others were scared, and eventually became an indisputable market leader.

Courage is also required in proposition development. Given the globally recognized low success rate for innovations or new products, it takes guts and a clear vision of market leadership to invest in research and development to develop innovative products with a high risk of failure. Some other brands are content to copy and mass customize. They are not interested in taking risks and so cannot savour the thrill of victory.

Cutting edge creativity is required to effectively communicate the brand values and benefits of value proposition packages to prospects. Normal threadbare and safe creativity resides in the realm of the ordinary. Breaking parity in a cluttered environment requires some boldness to embrace cutting edge creativity that breaks the norm and pushes the brand to the hedge. Bold concepts, bold formats, bold executions, hallmark market leaders. To be big and bold is a mantra with market leaders when it comes to engaging their customers and building brand affinity.

Market leaders define practice by what they do. They set category or industry standards. One of such ways is the redefinition of route to market. Market leaders change the game by creating new routes to market that leave competitors breathless. One of the ways to discomfit competition is by changing the rules of engagement. Changing market structure and trade remuneration structure can significantly upset market equilibrium to the aggressor brand's advantage.

Availability at every point of purchase is critical, especially if the business chooses to compete for volume market leadership. This calls for both depth and width of distribution and significant investment in tools, systems and processes. It also demands significant head count within the sales force either as direct staff or indirect staff members. A market leader can also differentiate in the way its logistics is managed from inbound to outbound to ensure that the pipeline is always filled and issues of stock-out do not occur. Stock-outs give room for trials of competing brands, which could lead to conversion. To prevent accidental conversions therefore, availability at every point of purchase becomes a must.

Internal efficiencies that deliver savings that

Stingy brands end up as idea incubators for aggressive brands focused on effective investments to gain share.

can be passed on to the consumers are a critical lever that can be leveraged by a brand in pursuit of volume market leadership. Lean and fit operations that translate to lower costs of production can be used as the strategy to deliver good quality at affordable prices that will generate volume push when the savings are passed on to the consumer.

Stingy brands cannot make the list of market leaders when it comes to marketing investments. While wastage is not advocated, effective budget is required to drive excellent marketing ideas. Stingy brands end up as idea incubators for aggressive brands focused on effective investments to gain share. Brilliant marketing campaigns with insufficient budget to deliver effective frequencies in exposure end up as dumb campaigns with frustrated writers. A certain level of investment is required to guarantee effective reach at the right frequency. Well-planned and executed brand campaigns backed with sufficient budget gives the brand gravitas. Investing in innovative media platforms that confers clout on the brand can also break media clutter.

Sometimes, brands can use the media to create impressions and manage perceptions as market leaders when indeed they are not. Such brands aggressively communicate market leadership intentions, but do so in very smart ways that give off the impression of reality. Such perception management conditions people's thinking about the brand. If the brand is strategically focused enough and scales up its services or product portfolio to deliver on its expressed intentions, the market can forgive its claims and possible puffery. Such campaigns of intentions can also destroy the brand if it fails to consistently deliver.

Big brands do big things in big ways. Ambitious brands do the same. Such brands send signals to the market about their ambitions. This may be expressed in their customer engagement strategies and the kind of sponsorship platforms they invest in. A young brand that chooses to invest in sponsorship properties like, the

Barclays English Premier League, the Champions League, or the World Cup, as a platform for engaging her customers has clearly indicated its ambitions and intentions.

True market leadership is not measured in intentions. It is also not measured in perceptions. It is measured in numbers. It is measured in value. The amount of returns either in customer count, volume purchase, and/or margin percentage, is what determines true leadership. If a brand has leadership in perception, it is an asset that can be leveraged for volume or value growth. If it is not leveraged for real growth, it is a waste. Perception and intentions not leveraged is insanity. Hard numbers in volume sales, strong cash flow, and/or significant margin advantage is sanity.

THOUGHT LEADERSHIP AS PRELUDE TO MARKET LEADERSHIP: THE INSIGHT COMMUNICATIONS STORY

Sustainable market leadership in very competitive categories is not a casual process. It is driven by clear visions translated into actionable and measurable initiatives consistently fine-tuned for continued relevance, but excellently executed. This vision is anchored on thought leadership. A brand in the Nigerian advertising industry that places absolute premium on thought leadership and has remained an indisputable market leader is Insight Communications.

Having identified the importance of highly skilled excellent talents in the delivery of great advertising that build market leading brands, the dearth of core professionals in the industry, and the fact that Nigerian universities were not turning out fit-for-purpose graduates for the advertising and marketing communication industry, the Troyka Group, owners of Insight Communications, formally started a traineeship academy initiative in the late 1980s christened, "Insight Management Traineeship Programme"

171

(IMTP). This scheme has graduated nineteen sets of marketing communications professionals. The program has since been re-christened, Troyka Executive Traineeship Programme'.

The IMTP is exclusively designed to absorb and train fresh graduates. However, it has a variant: executive-manager academy. This serves as the nursery bed for nurturing mid-career entrants into the profession, through structured conversion and immersion training programmes and exposures. The background idea is to develop an orientation towards particular ways of thinking, working and overall corporate culture (the 'Insight-way').

This first of its kind management traineeship scheme has since turned the organization into the factory of excellent talents, not just for Troyka Group and the advertising industry, but also for the entire marketing industry.

The selection process is painstaking. Young and malleable outstanding candidates across all disciplines, but preferably the humanities, art and single subject sciences get selected via a rigorous process. These candidates must display innate overt creativity, leadership competence, confidence, adaptability, trainability, strong passion for advertising, marketing communications, and Insight Communications in particular. Special attention is paid to strong middle class values, foremost of which are stability, loyalty, fidelity, truthfulness, integrity, honor and commitment to purpose. These are added criteria for selecting this group that the organization considers as the future leaders of her business.

This one-year intensive traineeship programme takes on a minimum of ten intakes each year, and employs a combination of Class work, Lectures, Seminars, Simulation Classes, Presentations, Role-plays, Brainstorming sessions, and Book Reviews. Candidates are also sent on Attachment in different departments/units, Member Companies, Client Companies, and Third-party supplier companies. Mentoring is also done by the senior staff members.

Each candidate then concludes with a specific task or Project Paper.

The IMTP and its executive managers academy has produced over five hundred professionals over its period of existence. Some of these professionals are the leading lights in the Nigerian advertising and marketing communications Industry today. Others are notable icons in core marketing management across industries. Her pool of Alumni membership is an enviable list of CEOs of leading advertising agencies and senior marketing management executives.

The greatest beneficiary of this scheme is Insight Communications herself. Annually, the agency gets the pick of the crème of the talents that walk through the scheme. These talents are deployed on the agency's businesses with excellent results. The agency has therefore, consistently attracted and won blue chip accounts that over the years have conferred undisputable leadership on her. Fresh thinking from new intakes nurtured in a structured environment continuously enhances the organization's robust capacity for consistent thought leadership. Her market leadership over the years is living proof.

EPILOGUE

THE DIGITAL AND BIG DATA AGE: THE ICE IS MELTING!

The Digital revolution sweeping the whole world is redefining the marketing management practice in form and fundamentally enhancing content. Technological advancement and breakthrough thinking in the area of data sourcing, storage, analysis and interpretation for strategy has gained relevance and prominence. At the realm of the Logic side of marketing, technology is helping to better access and understand both transactional data and formal research data in near real time and sometimes real time.

This enhances deeper insight and engenders faster and smarter decision making that can fundamentally affect business performance. Marketers now have tools that aid the product development process, consumer data and insight generation, effective macro and micro segmentation, trade channel understanding and optimization, communication and consumer engagement platforms optimization etc.

Wastage occasioned by the difficulty of real time data availability and tools for analyzing the same for insights have consistently

174

gone on the decline. This has challenged the 50% wastage theory. Tools now exist to measure returns on marketing investments. Planning in the dark, guess works, strategic gambles and village intelligence as foundations for strategy are fast losing currency.

Within the marketing media environment, practice is becoming much more scientific. Channels and platforms can now be pre-tested. Real time data is now accessible for tweaking strategy and optimizing spend. Advancement in broadcast technology now provides digital signatures that may ultimately erase an entire industry sector; broadcast media monitoring, as it gains full acceptance. The planned digitization of the broadcast industry would force current technologies into obsolescence. The digital media has exploded with increased broadband access. Full marketing campaigns and online consumer engagements now get planned, executed and monitored via the digital platforms. The present has become digital. It is no longer a futuristic phenomenon.

The magic dimension of marketing has not been spared by the torrent of technological innovations in the digital and big data space either. These innovations are enhancing the creative process, the ideation process and the communication process with direct impact on output quality and speed. Data, logic or digitalization may not replace the magic. Humans are still the end recipient of the product of logic. Their purchase decisions are more often than not emotional especially if the desire is a very valuable item. The evolution is however fundamental and nothing will be left the same way ever again. This reality demands a changing marketer. There is a need for re-skilling, retooling and significant shifts in paradigm. It is time to unlearn some skills and pick up new ones. The game is changing. The ice is melting! Marketing starts and ends with the consumer. That consumer is in flight. If you must nail this moving target, you must keep moving. You must keep changing.

Notes

9 780985 081591